Wake Up!

Stop Sabotaging Your Happiness and Your Success

Wake Up!

Stop Sabotaging Your Happiness
and Your Success

Anne Astilleros

FINDHORN PRESS

Published in 2017 by Findhorn Press, Scotland

ISBN 978-1-84409-738-8

A CIP record for this title is available from the British Library.

Edited by Nicky Leach
Cover design by José Antonio
Interior design by Damian Keenan
Printed and bound in the USA

DISCLAIMER

The information in this book (in print and electronic media)
is given in good faith and is neither intended to diagnose any
physical or mental condition nor to serve as a substitute for
informed medical advice or care.
Please contact your health professional for medical advice and
treatment. Neither author nor publisher can be held liable by
any person for any loss or damage whatsoever which may arise
from the use of this book or any of the information therein.

Published by
Findhorn Press
117-121 High Street,
Forres IV36 1AB,
Scotland, UK

t +44 (0)1309 690582
f +44 (0)131 777 2711
e info@findhornpress.com
www.findhornpress.com

Contents

Preface 7

Introduction 9

Principles of My Philosophy 11

PART ONE: Remember Who You Are 13

1   And What If You Had Simply Forgotten? 15
2   Do You Dare to Rediscover Yourself? 18
3   You, and Everything Else That Exists, Are Energy 24
4   You Are Both Light and Darkness, and That Is Fine 32
5   The Trinity in You 37
6   The Promises You Made Before You Were Born 45

PART TWO: Be Grateful To Your Parents 51

7   You Chose Your Parents in Order to Remember
    What Not to Do 53
8   How Do You Sabotage Yourself? 60
9   The Roles We Adopt 65
10 Messages We Have Chosen to Believe 79
11 Do What I Failed to Do 82
12 Forgive Them 88
13 The Inherent Guilt in You 93
14 Stop Punishing Yourself 99

PART THREE: Remember How To Use Your Power
To Create Your Life 103

15 Claim Responsibility 105
16 Your Mission and Your Purpose 113
17 Universal Principles at Your Service 121
18 Guide Your Thoughts 128
19 Ask Your Being 133
20 When the Ego Attacks 141

21	Your Emotions Are Your Best Indicator	146
22	Heal Your Fear	153
23	Cast Away the Sadness in Your Life	158

PART FOUR: To Evolve Is Your Sole Responsibility 165

24	Being Happy Is an Altruistic Act	167
25	Relationships as the Motor of Evolution	173
26	Your Job at the Service of Your Happiness	179
27	Education for Happiness	184
28	You Promised Yourself to Take Care of Your Vehicle	189
29	You Promised Yourself to Care for the Planet	198

PART FIVE: Make Peace With Death And Enjoy Your Life 201

30	Death as a Continuation of Your Path	203
31	Your Life is Multidimensional	209
32	Enjoy Your Life	213
33	Global Consciousness	217
34	Daring to Be Happy Means… Choosing to Feel Happy	220

| | Glossary | 222 |
| | About the Author | 224 |

Preface

I met Anne ten years ago at a small seminar where she had been invited to speak. Until that day, my entire life had revolved around the search for a solution that would help ease people's suffering, a suffering that we all feel but don't often speak about. I suppose that a childhood fraught with depression and malaise had naturally rendered me predisposed to this longing, this search, which in my case became the epicenter of my life. I needed proof that it was also possible to be genuine and happy here on this planet.

In my quest, I pursued studies and obtained various degrees, as a psychologist, psychotherapist, life coach, and family constellation facilitator. I learned how to use a variety of techniques and methods. I worked with "masters," therapists, shamans, and psychologists. I traveled intensively across the continents, with the sole purpose of finding this "something" that would facilitate the way to genuine Happiness; this "something" that would alleviate the emptiness that we all, to a greater or lesser extent, feel.

The day that I heard Anne speak for the first time in that seminar I knew I had found it. From the very first minute, all of us present were captivated by her powerful and natural joy, by her presence and simplicity, by a kind of glow that seemed to fill the entire room. Her gaze transmitted Peace, transmitted this "something" that I had been seeking for so long. Much to my surprise and delight, her speech was just as simple and powerful as her presence. Finally, I had found a genuine person—a person who had not forgotten who she was, what her purpose was; someone who reminded us to stop looking outside ourselves, when everything, absolutely everything that we need we already possess, naturally, within.

Anne's words resonated strikingly in my depths like great truths that I already knew (rediscovered) and that were simply waiting to be awakened. I had the sensation that Anne was speaking to each and every participant in the very heart of our Being. In that moment I knew we would be friends, and I can assure you that when I decide on something I can be very, very persistent.

Anne, at that time, was a diamond in the rough, a source still untapped. She had worked here and there, offering individual sessions when people asked her to, but she had never seriously considered speaking publicly about her way of seeing and feeling, and especially about her special connection to the Universe. In the course of human history, there have been very few human beings who have communicated so clearly and directly with the Source and who, in addition, have dared to speak of it publicly. The very rare exceptions who have not forgotten who they are and where they have come from have generally ended up being rejected, treated like lunatics, or simply eliminated. It doesn't surprise me that at the time Anne had qualms about publicly conveying her message.

Nevertheless, here we are, in early 2017, and her book is done. The work that you have in your hands is the summary of her powerful philosophy of life. For her, they are no more than inklings and broad brushstrokes of Reality, whereas for us, they constitute genuine discoveries, striking and revelatory. They allow us not only to resume our lives but to raise them to any level of Happiness and satisfaction we desire, both on this and other planes of existence, now and in our vital future experiences, in this and in all other universes to which we will head.

Note: In this book, I serve as a translator from Anne's language, springing directly from the Source and not always easy to understand, to a language more readily accessible to all. I apologize in advance for transforming something so beautiful and pure for the sake of comprehension, but I am certain that, in this case, the end does justify the means.

For Anne, precision in words is fundamental, and it is for this reason that we include a glossary at the back of the book to clarify the meaning of certain terms that she tends to employ in unconventional ways. For instance, you will see that she capitalizes certain words, investing them with a special meaning, different from the norm: Being, Light, Ignorance, and so forth.

I dare, and I'm happy. What about you?

— **Victoria Vinuesa**
  Writer, screenwriter, and psychologist,
  among other things.

Introduction

*Your Being holds a secret that gives you the Power
to transform your life forever.*

You, like each one of us, were born with the innate Power to experience a life of Happiness, Success, and Well-Being. So what is still preventing you from feeling genuinely happy in each moment and in each facet of your life? There is only one cause: your Obliviousness.

The Being, once incarnated in its human body, forgets the true meaning of its earthly experience. Not only has it forgotten the goal for which it decided to incarnate itself and the promises that it made to itself, but it has also forgotten Who it is in its Essence and what its true Divine nature is. It has forgotten its Creator, Mother-Father.

My purpose in writing this book is to help you to remember, so that you can recapture your Happiness and your lost motivation, resume your communication with your own Knowledge, alleviate your sense of guilt and malaise, improve your relationships, and triumph for Love in everything you set out to do.

As a human Being attentive to my Knowledge, it has always been clear to me that it is my duty to share my particular, although completely simple and natural, way of seeing and perceiving Life with this "unreal" world. A few years back, my friend and fellow writer Victoria Vinuesa asked me the question that I had heard so many times before: "When do you intend to write a book that shares with the people of this planet your philosophy of liberation, the one you have come here to teach?"

Victoria was persistent. She even offered to help me write the book, because she knew that, for me, it would not be easy to capture in human words the language of my Knowledge, the essential Knowledge that lies in all of us, much less in English.

The day Victoria urged me to communicate my philosophy to the world, I felt my Happiness responding of its own accord: "Yes, yes. Tell her, tell Anne. Help her to set Me free and disseminate Me, thus helping others to also awaken to their own Happiness."

Human language has countless words but very few that can transmit the Essence of Life. I asked myself, too, if the words that I was to make use of would convey the joy and simplicity that characterize me; if they would be received as I intended them, when we all know that one is responsible for what one says, not for how others will hear or interpret it.

If I have decided to open a small door to my inner depths and approach you through this book, it is with the sole purpose of calling your attention to and helping you awaken to your own Reality, to your purpose, to the promise you made to Yourself and to your Creating Parents before embarking on your journey; so you can recognize "I AM" in you, your luminous part, that unconditional True Love creator of your Being, the inexhaustible Source, that is Happiness in you.

You need to wake up.

Allow me to state that I am not a scientist, nor am I religious or "spiritual" in the conventional sense of the term. I simply speak from the expression of Knowledge, the same one that resides inside you and inside each person.

Always keep in mind that there is nothing that I do, say, see, or manifest that you cannot equally do, say, see, or manifest in your life. I'm not interested in followers; only in free people excited by their own Evolution. REMEMBER: Your sole master, the only valid master for you, resides inside you.

Peace and Joy
I = Anne

Principles of
My Philosophy

1. You are an eternal and multidimensional energy Being.
2. You have a dual nature: You are both Light (Creating Essence) and darkness (a space in which to experience and evolve).
3. Your Being has one purpose: to make you into the alchemist who transforms "its" darkness into Light along its own path.
4. To manifest your Happiness is your duty and your sole responsibility.
5. Before being born into this body, you chose a way in which you would fulfill your purpose in this life: your mission.
6. You promised yourself that you would become the alchemist of your life, that is, the one who invariably illuminates the darkness in its path.
7. Darkness, on this planet, galaxy, and universe, is more abundant and more present than Light. It is your responsibility to illuminate it.
8. You are a co-creating Being of worlds and experiences.
9. You are surrounded by an infinite number of energy currents, more or less luminous, to which you connect according to your thoughts, actions, and emotional state. These currents will determine the quality of your daily life and will create your path.
10. Your emotions, sensations, and thoughts shape your reality.
11. The Creating Essence offers you its Universal Principles to help you create your life according to your desires.
12. You are the only one responsible for your unique capital: your own Happiness. Thanks to this capital, you hold the power to create all of your experiences.
13. Your Creating Parents (God) love you unconditionally and do not need to forgive you for your mistakes; however, you need to forgive yourself.
14. You are not, nor will you ever be, "perfect" as a human being, and it's alright. You should not punish yourself for it, but instead, start to make the best changes for your evolution.

15. You were born with an intrinsic guilt that is a product of the dark memories of your experiential Being. Forgiving yourself is your duty.
16. The root of all human problems is oblivion, the forgetting of Who we are in our Essence, of our true nature. This obliviousness leads us to identify ourselves with the manufacturers of our bodies, Mom and Dad, thereby turning our backs on our Creating Parents: God, Father-Mother .
17. Your Life, not this earthly experience that you call life, is eternal and multidimensional.
18. This human life is merely one stop along your evolving path, called eternal.
19. Your death is nothing more than the abandonment of your human body to continue your experimental path in other places in other bodies adapted to those places that you choose to use.
20. Once you've left this body, Light, as an expression of Love, is the only fuel you need for traveling to other more luminous worlds, those that are filled with joy.
21. The Light that you generate in this life will determine your Happiness and well-being in the next.
22. The Beings that upon their death have not generated Love, that is to say, sufficient light to move to happier worlds (levels of evolution) have options; for example, to be reincarnated in a human body (thus "repeating the lesson") or remain in the atomic body state (those you call ghosts), until they gather enough Light to continue on their path.
23. Your relationships, especially the ones with your physical parents, are your best human base for evolution. They offer you the best options and examples to increasing your Happiness (Light).
24. You promised yourself not to repeat the dark behaviors that you already used in other lives.
25. You chose your physical parents, Mom and Dad, in order to remember what *not* to do.
26. You promised yourself to become the "master" of your biological parents.
27. Your Being manifests itself in your person through your ego, your "I", and your Heart.
28. Your "I" is your free will. It decides to whom to pay attention: your dark ego or your ever-luminous Heart.
29. The ego is your great ally (motor) in your Evolution.

Part One

Remember Who You Are

CHAPTER 1

And What If You Had Simply Forgotten?

The Being, eternal co-creator and son of the Essence Father and Mother, once incarnated, will have to awaken to its new human reality. Failing this, as a human being, it will feel mortal, unhappy, and lost.

One day, a droplet of the Creating Essence is released from the Absolute to experiment with an infinite array of experiences, inhabiting an infinite number of places, adopting an infinite quantity of different forms, all of which have one single purpose: to allow Love, transformer of darkness, to reign.

This droplet is, also, You.

And you ... Do you dare to be happy?

Does it not seem contradictory to you that one should have to dare to do something as natural as being and feeling happy?

Come along with me in this book, and you will discover why daring to be happy is, in reality, a feat for the brave. But remember that I'm talking about bravery as an expression of the Heart, not the strength of muscle.

The Root of All Human Problems: Forgetting

The root of all human problems is forgetting Who we are in our Essence, in forgetting our Perfection for the sole benefit of our bodies.

We are like sleepwalkers moving through life oblivious to ourselves, to our Reality, and to our timelessly loving Identity.

Allow me to tell you a brief story.

There was once a King who happily governed a kingdom of great beauty and health, where affection, respect, and joy reigned supreme among its people. A passing visitor, drawn to the kingdom by its goodness, met with the King and spoke to him of a not-too-distant planet where the inhabitants seemed submerged in a profound and interminable sadness. He told the King that both the air and the water of the place had been gradually contaminated by its own inhabitants and that they spent long hours of each day doing unfulfilling work for a sole purpose: survival.

The King, astounded, asked him a single question, "By chance, are these Beings lacking a heart?"

"Of course not" replied the visitor. "In fact, when it stops people die."

"In that case it's impossible that they would have strayed to that extent," the King said.

Without thinking twice, the ruler resolved to go there himself and help those distant brothers to remember the power of their hearts. Yes, he would remind them of the importance of reawakening the Beauty of Life and would help them rediscover the Reason to exist and the importance of remaining in their Joy. Determined, he embarked on the journey astride his winged horse.

As he descended toward the planet shrouded in darkness, he was struck by the density of the air that invaded that atmosphere. It was stifling, and soon he began to have trouble breathing it. He dismounted his winged horse and began walking through the sad streets of a crowded and noisy city. The people, devoid of expression, looked at him without seeing him, or without much interest. They seemed to be in a kind of trance caused by their forgetting; yes, the obliviousness that they were also the beloved children of the infinite and unconditionally Loving Creation.

Something in the dense air made the well-intentioned visitor dizzy. He leaned on a wall to avoid falling, and suddenly, looking around, he, too, began to forget. He could no longer remember where he had come from or why he had come, and worse still, he couldn't remember who he was. The King, anguished and confused, didn't know what to do.

Gradually becoming himself a sleepwalker, he started imitating others, behaving like them.

Weeks later, the inhabitants of his kingdom, alarmed by the absence of their beloved King, sent a retinue of his most valiant knights, the Knights of the Awakened Heart, so that they might help him in what seemed an arduous task.

The Knights of the Awakened Heart traveled to that planet in search of their King. Protected by thick masks, they avoided having to breathe the poisoned air. Following a long search, they found him under the rays of a blazing sun. Exhausted and saddened, he was tilling the earth with great effort.

The knights, surprised and confused, tried to make him remember who he was and told him the reason why he had decided to come to this place. But the King did not believe what these men were saying. His reality, the only one that existed for him now, was that one.

It took him some time to remember Who he really was and recover his forgotten reason to exist and his Joy, and he needed to use his dormant Heart once more in order to accomplish it, but to the great delight of his people, he succeeded!

And what if you, too, had simply forgotten who you really are?

CHAPTER 2

Do You Dare to Rediscover Yourself?

True alchemy consists in transforming darkness
with your own Light through your actions,
with the aid of your original luminous capital.

We've been taught that only what we can perceive with our limited human vision exists. Anything that is not perceived with the humanly accepted senses is forgotten, set aside, or socially marginalized. Humans insist on using the mind for everything, as if it were a computer, allowing it to take the lead on other functions, even their own feelings and emotions. But Reality requires more observation—even contemplation—than rational comprehension. The human being is equipped to observe, feel, perceive, understand, and learn in order to survive and has constant access to his own Knowledge, matchless treasure inherited from the Creation itself, Father-Mother in each one of us. Thinking is far from being his only function.

You are a Precious Being, Rich and purely energetic-vibrational, which at a certain moment on its journey—called eternal—through this Universe, decided to make a stop on the planet called Earth. As an evolutionary Being experiencing Itself, your nature is twofold: You are Light that crosses a darkness for which you are responsible, and you are a luminous core (the very droplet of the Creating Essence), which finds itself invariably surrounded, to a greater or lesser degree, by darkness.

Your sole purpose on your universal journey is to evolve; that is, to illuminate the darkness, not to identify with it, in the course of your multi-dimensional experience.

We all have the same purpose recorded in our Interior: to return Home.

Before going any farther, however, permit me to clarify what I'm referring to when I speak of Light and darkness. Light is Love in all the manifestations that we know: joy, well-being, peace, eagerness, richness, friendship, kindness (toward and to yourself first, and not for approval or to be liked by others, which would make you a beggar of love), and so on.

Darkness is the lack, not the absence of, expressed Light. Darkness is nothing more than the other side of the luminous Essence. It is Essence as yet unexposed to experiences of Love.

The Birth of Your Being

Allow me to speak to you of the birth of your Being, that which inhabits your body at the present moment. Be aware that I am not speaking of the birth of the physical body; the body you identify with every time you look in the mirror and experience the gaze of others; the body that serves as your vehicle and with which you have until now identified yourself to a greater or lesser degree. Instead, I am speaking of the eternally Loving Being that inhabits and gives life to it.

One day, many lives ago now, a droplet of the Creating Essence (God) was released from the source of the Absolute in order to live out a long—called eternal—journey through this and other universes.

From the moment in which this droplet of the Essence was released from the source of the Absolute and began to move away, it also began to gradually be surrounded by a deepening and dense darkness. It was in this precise moment that, seeing itself surrounded by a great lack of Light, the droplet resolved to become the alchemist that as it passed would invariably illuminate the cold and dark time-space, on the paths of its eternal journey.

That very moment represents the birth of your unique Being, indivisible and ready to be incarnated.

Between these two states, Light and darkness, unconditionally appears that gift, as divine as unequaled, that gift that each and every one, without exception, call I. I is the free will, the driver of your multidimensional experience, the one that you mention so much every day, and that on the other hand you seem to ignore as a perfect and often as an unwelcome stranger

Did you know that you are the true and only alchemist of your life?

Your Eternal Evolutionary Journey
as a Provider of Love

As a Being detached from the Creating Source, you exist with a sole Purpose: to transform the darkness you pass through into Light in the course of your myriad universal experiences; those which you call lives. For you, expanding Love is something natural since you are It.

For your Purpose, you employ different "bodies" adapted to the different places in the Universe (planets, stars, galaxies, and so on) where you decide to carry out this expansion and perform the alchemy that entails entering into matter (the body) and living with it. At the present moment, you are using a human body to inhabit and to keep on manifesting our Creating Parents on planet Earth.

The Birth of Your Material Body

One day, you as a Being without a material body who had already embarked on its evolving journey, and finding yourself between the two experiences, encountered the planet Earth and decided to make a stop on it.

You looked at the planet with tenderness and unconditional Love. You saw it disturbed, sad, completely polluted, and sickened by its own inhabitants—inhabitants who were convinced of their status as orphans and of being punished to a greater or lesser extent by a severe god that they themselves had invented.

It was at that moment that you decided to incarnate in order to awaken those Beings that were already human to the hard oblivion of their infinitely loving Reality. You wanted to offer them a new reflection of their own Light. You decided this as a result of the Knowledge you held, as a Being still free from matter. You decided that you would become embodied in order to share your inexhaustible Heart with those inhabitants, your Brothers. At that moment you felt sure, because you knew that you could interact, express, and relate to all of them.

Eagerly, you made two solemn promises. On the one hand, you promised to continue evolving by not falling into the darkness you had already experienced; in other words, you would be the alchemist who transforms the darkness as he crosses its path. On the other hand, at the moment in which you chose the manufacturers of the body you were to inhabit, those whom you call Mom and Dad, you made a solemn promise to respect them and not emulate them in their dark side, their negative behavior guided by their egos and by the collective ego of this planet.

At that moment, just before your incarnation, you were and felt yourself to be powerful and capable of keeping your promises. You were the droplet of Creating Essence and possessed all of the tools to convert your experience on this planet into a genuine experimentation of Happiness and enjoyment. You were the Power itself, capable of creating the life of your choosing. You knew the universal principles that govern Life and were willing to use them in your favor throughout your earthly sojourn as a human being.

The Material Trap

To manifest yourself as a person on Earth you needed a vehicle, a human body, and for this purpose you chose a man and a woman who would manufacture your body, those whom today you call Mom and Dad. Thus far, everything was at Peace, and all was going according to plan.

However, the Being, once incarnated into a physical body, offspring of the matter it has chosen, faces two possible scenarios.

FIRST SCENARIO: The Being and its human body maintain a fluent communication and a relationship from Love. Albeit natural, this scenario, in reality, is extremely rare.

SECOND SCENARIO: The person inhabited by the Being does not identify with It but with the manufacturers of his body: his biological parents. Although these may be excellent people, they are just that: people, not gods. The Being, therefore, feels trapped. The communication between the Being and its vehicle (its body) is difficult, complicated, or is even lost completely.

This second scenario is the most frequent, if not the only one existing on our planet. The human being estranged from its Creating Parents—God, the Source of Love—identifies itself, in general, with its manufacturers: Mom and Dad.

To put it another way, it's as if your person had gradually forgotten about You, the Being that it carries within. While you identify with your physical parents and try to live your life according to pre-established human norms, you forget that evolution is only possible when it springs from Love, and that this is the true reason for which you decided to become incarnated, your only reason to exist. You forget that your passage on this planet is temporary.

The very moment you forget to live, you begin to survive.

The Taxi Metaphor

Let me explain this apparent nonsense with a metaphor. Imagine a taxi in which there is a soundproof window between the driver and the passenger. The passenger has a special GPS device, a GPS that leads one only to express and experience Happiness. The driver has an intercom which, when activated, allows communication between both.

The one driving is the taxi driver, but the one deciding where to go is the passenger assisted by his internal GPS. The car, however, only follows the orders and directions issued by the driver.

In this metaphor, the car is your material body, the driver is your mind, the passenger is your Being, and his expression is what we all call I.

What would happen if the driver, only aware of external events, forgot that he had a passenger in the car? Imagine, then, that the passenger in the backseat, realizing that the driver had lost his way and was straying from the path to Happiness, tried to make himself heard, while the taxi driver, oblivious to his passenger, had not activated his intercom and could not hear him.

That is precisely what happens in people. Our vehicle is a solid and material body. The dense and heavy material of which our bodies are made closes us in and slow us down. The person, cheated by his ego-mind, forgets about his Identity, forgets about his I.

The Being will not be able to manifest itself and the car, your body, will be led exclusively by the driver, by the mind disconnected from your Knowledge.

As a result, we sense that we are missing something. And what do we do when we sense or believe that "something" is missing, even unconsciously? What we do is try to find it externally, in others. Already from our childhood, we are like taxis driven by the mental patterns of others. From then on, the false personalities we copied from others continue to grow.

What we call personality is a far cry from our true Identity, manifest and respectful of our Being.

Recover Your Identity

Haven't you ever had the feeling or realized that some of your forms of behavior and ways of thinking are, in reality, foreign to you? In other words, a feeling of not knowing why you're behaving a certain way, as if to say, "I don't know what I'm doing; this is not me."

In general, from childhood, we identify with our physical parents or elders, gradually forgetting our own and unique Identity. The child turns its back on the Identity with which it was born in order to be accepted in its environment, improvising, day after day, a superficial personality estranged from its Purpose. That borrowed superficial personality is the one that generally expresses itself in our life; it is the deaf taxi driver who is guided by others.

Re-Establish Contact With Your Passenger

The purpose of this book, and of my entire method and philosophy, is precisely this: to help the driver remember that he is carrying a passenger—a passenger endowed with a marvelous GPS. All that's needed is for the driver to re-establish contact with this passenger in order to be led to those paths most disposed to Love, to be given the best chances of Happiness and total well-being, regardless of the paths it may choose to illuminate or create along the way.

You are not alone! You, too, can re-establish contact with your passenger and be guided by its inner GPS: your unique and precious I.

Dare, and be happy!

CHAPTER 3

You, and Everything Else That Exists, Are Energy

You may close your eyes, turn your back on yourself,
but you will never be able to override your Being,
its Essence in you.

For some time now, quantum physics has taught us that in this Universe, everything, absolutely everything, is energy. It is entirely composed of more or less luminous energy. The physical atoms are made of vortexes of energy that vibrate and spin incessantly on themselves. Matter and human consciousness are energy, and they are interconnected. As surprising as it may seem to the sometimes inflexible human mind, human consciousness has the power to influence the behavior of matter and restructure it.

The less luminous energy has a lower rate of vibration and manifests itself in denser material forms. In contrast, everything that is light and less dense, such as light, air, steam, rainbows, or the aurora borealis, is composed of more luminous energy of a faster vibration.

Look for a moment at your hands. These hands, which you perceive as something solid and definite, in reality are nothing more than the sum of energy particles vibrating at lower speeds. If these particles were to start vibrating at a higher rate, you would see something shaped like your hands but made of millions of infinitesimal lights, and if the velocity were high enough, you would cease to see your hands completely.

Matter that is denser and heavier, such as the matter that makes up our bodies and the things we perceive as solid, is made of slow and less luminous energy. The particles that constitute these objects vibrate slowly, and it is precisely this low velocity that causes us to see these objects as solid and well defined. It is simply an illusion of our limited human sensory system.

What an interesting subject to add to our kids' school curriculum! Wouldn't you agree?

The Vision of Light Energy

We are all born with the ability to see beyond the contours of things we perceive as well defined; indeed, we are all capable of seeing the lighter energy that our eyes do not perceive as solid.

If you've ever had the opportunity to live with a baby in its first months of life, you will have observed how there are moments when its gaze appears to be focused on something in the air that has seized its attention—something that is utterly invisible to you. Have you noticed how they stare into space, sometimes for long minutes, looking at something adults cannot see?

At birth, babies enjoy a richer spectrum of vision. During the first months of life, they don't easily make out the contours of material objects, which have a slower vibration. Their visual world is composed almost exclusively of multicolored, light energy that is in constant flux.

Now, you may be asking yourself why it is, then, that as they grow up, people lose this natural vision of a richer reality. Have you noticed how adults and children older than two years, who interact with babies, always try to get them to focus their attention on some object or person? I'm sure you're familiar with the scene in which someone shows an object to a baby, trying to get its attention and saying, "Look! Look!" Or the biological mother who gets up close to her baby and looks straight into its eyes, trying to get all of its attention. The baby is constantly surrounded by older people who try to divert its gaze so that it focuses exclusively on the denser and heavier objects.

Generally, adults only give importance to what can be seen with the human eye, what is totally solid or of a nature dense enough to be seen, such as smoke, vapor, or the colors of twilight. Thus, through interactions with adults in their environment, babies gradually set aside and keep out of sight their natural capacity for experiencing higher vibrational energy, with the sole purpose of being accepted and recognized by the adult world. It is merely a question of survival!

Little by little, babies lose interest in their own natural vision, which their Being still offers them and which allows them to see all the things the adult world can no longer see. It was in this way that you too ended up losing interest in your vision, ignoring it in exchange for recognition from those people who constituted your new world. Nevertheless, it is possible to gradually recover this vision of lighter energy, and quite natural for you as a human being.

Infants with whom I have had the opportunity to live in this earthly experience give me a smile of relief when they realize that I, too, see this "something" that is invisible to other adults. The affectionate bond created in these moments can be very endearing.

The Light and the Darkness

Let me make two things clear before proceeding: In Reality as I perceive it, Light and darkness are not two independent entities; rather, Light inhabits the darkness, and darkness surrounds Light. But for ease of reading and comprehension throughout this book, we will view them as separate. Secondly, the Light I'm referring to in this book has nothing to do with the light that your eyes see shining from the sun, glowing in a bulb, or sparking in a match.

Light is the energy with the fastest vibration known in the Universe. It is movement. Light is a manifestation of Love, which creates experiences through your thoughts and behavior. Love is the Supreme Intelligence, and manifests itself in your daily life through you and your Heart. This manifested Light is what we call Happiness; its source is Love.

Darkness complements Light. It is the energy with the lowest rate of vibration. It is dense and static. In reality, darkness is nothing more than the other side of the loving and luminous Essence—the side of the Essence that has not yet been experienced and transformed by Light; that is to say, darkness is as yet untouched by luminous experiences.

Darkness lacks the constant expression of Light, and its emotional manifestation is fear.

Yes, as surprising as it may seem, darkness has nothing to do with evil. Evil is what we do with that darkness when we pass through it; that is to say, it represents our failure to fulfill our only duty—to bestow love upon it.

Choose Your Chalk

We can picture darkness as an enormous blank chalkboard on which we can write with pieces of chalk (thoughts, emotions, and actions) of all colors. You are free to choose how you would like to draw on your chalkboard: with pieces of beautifully colored chalk chosen from your Heart, or if you have not yet awakened your inner Light and grown with it, perhaps you are blindly drawing with the darkest chalk that your ego instructs you to. What result do you think will come from drawing with black chalk on a black chalkboard?

As incredible as it may seem, darkness wants nothing more than for you to illuminate it; it wants you to express and expand your Love when passing through it.

Emotions Are Energy

Your emotions, like everything else in existence, are energy. Emotions characterized by slower vibrations, the dark ones, are those that provoke some sense of unease, pain, or unpleasant sensations, such as fear, impotence, frustration, guilt, jealousy, sadness, envy, boredom, apathy, and suspicion. Luminous emotions, on the other hand, are those that, when you choose to think and act from Love, awaken within you feelings of peace, trust, well-being, and every type of pleasant sensation, such as joy, compassion, tenderness, enthusiasm, excitement, and so on.

Emotions that emanate from Love vibrate freely, are lighter and more expansive, and awaken Happiness in You. Dark emotions, conversely, vibrate slowly, are denser and heavier, and therefore make you feel miserable in yourself.

Popular language itself is a faithful reflection of this reality. Are you familiar with expressions like "I have a heavy heart," "I have a lump in my throat," "That's a heavy load," and "That's a weight off my shoulders"?

Thoughts trigger your emotions and sensations, and they have the power to create your experiences. It is they and their vibratory energy that co-create your daily experiences.

The Energy Currents We Plug Into

In Reality as I perceive it, an infinite number of energy currents coexist in our space and circulate continuously around us. These currents range from the lightest, most luminous, and most brilliant all the way to the darkest, densest, and heaviest.

Each thought we have triggers in us a sensation or emotion that corresponds to a certain level of vibration. The energy wave that generates this emotion or sensation connects us instantaneously to a current of a similar energetic vibrational level. In this way, if the thought has been generated by the Light of your Heart, you will connect to a luminous current of well-being and feel happy when doing so. But if the thought is generated from your ever-dark ego, and you do nothing to change it, you will connect to a dark energy current, one that is of the same vibrational level as the thought you have authorized yourself to have. The result? You will feel bad.

You may be asking yourself, what are the practical consequences of connecting to one or another current? It would not be an exaggeration to state that the currents you choose to connect to will determine your life's path, your experiences, and your level of well-being in the more or less near future, and even beyond this human experience.

When we focus on a dark thought or an unpleasant situation, thus giving it more importance than the one necessary to change or transform it, we become immersed in the painful emotion that results; in this way, we connect ourselves to a type of current that automatically leads us to experience situations where we will re-create this emotion over and over again. On the other hand, if in the moment in which this negative situation arises, we consciously focus on a good thought, one that creates a more pleasant situation, a new emotion will follow, and in this way, what we will repeatedly create will also be pleasant.

What We Focus on We Create

As soon as we connect to any type of energy current, we immediately attract thoughts, emotions, situations, and circumstances of the same vibrational level. It's as if we are entering a specific dimension of existence.

To illustrate this with a metaphor, imagine you are in a movie theater with an infinite number of screens and an infinite number of movies to choose from. You have the Power to select which movie you wish to watch, and which type of emotions you wish to have. If you choose to treat yourself well and have a good time, you might choose to watch a romantic movie, a fantasy, an adventure, an inspirational story, or a comedy. If, on the other hand, you care to experience dark and uneasy emotions, you will no doubt choose to watch a movie depicting horror, terror, aggression, or violence. In either case, you choose the emotional experience you wish to plug into.

This is how it works in our lives, as well. The current to which we choose to connect ourselves is our way of selecting the emotions and situations we want to experience in our lives. If, for example, your thoughts are sad and you do nothing to change them, eventually you will connect yourself to an energy current of the same vibrational level as that sadness, and you will be choosing to live in a movie where sadness plays the leading role. On the other hand, if you choose thoughts that connect you to a current of action within Love, that will be the movie you are choosing to live in and the experience you co-create.

Suppose you have had an argument with a friend and feel angry. Minutes pass, even hours. Your anger persists because you have permitted the anger to fill your space, and therefore, you have connected yourself to a current of low energy. Due to this connection, you will enter a dimension of that vibrational level:

- The people around you will also react on this dark vibrational level.
- The situations you live through will cause you to re-create this dark vibration.
- The thoughts that occur to you will be dark, angry, filled with frustration, or maybe even revenge.
- The sensations and emotions will also be unpleasant, reinforcing your fall into darkness.
- And it will continue to be like this until you decide otherwise.

The Importance of Forgiveness

This is where forgiveness becomes vital. It doesn't matter what someone has done to you or what you may have done; allowing yourself to remain resentful or feel impotent with regard to that moment or situation will simply cause you to re-create that pain over and over again, and keep you immersed in a current of distress, perpetuating the pain and the discomfort. It's as if you were subjecting yourself to the same abuse time and time again.

Free Your Space

Allow me to offer another example drawn from real life that many people will recognize: online social networks.

Imagine that you "friend" ten people on a social network, and that of those ten people, three are always complaining, two favor sad and depressing posts, three others are great fans of horror movies, and the remaining two never post anything. Naturally, your newsfeed will only have sad, depressing, or horrible things to say. But what would happen if you decided to connect yourself to ten more people who were responsible, joyful, fun, courageous, and interesting? Well, at this point, at least half of the posts on your newsfeed would be cheerful and would bring a smile to your face. And what if you had only chosen well-meaning and cheerful friends from the very beginning? Exactly, 100 percent of the posts you received would make you smile.

The good news is that in the course of life, as through our social networks, you can select which types of emotions you wish to experience. In any given moment, you have the freedom to recognize that you've made a mistake and change direction. Just as on social networks, you can delete undesirable "friends," in your life you can free your space and allow yourself to enjoy new experiences.

The Message That Beats in Your Heart

The scientists at the Hearth Math Institute have demonstrated that the heart generates the largest electromagnetic field of any organ in our entire body, and that information regarding our emotions is codified within it and transmitted some distance out into the field surrounding the body. In this way, by changing our emotions and sensations, we will be altering the information of the electromagnetic field generated by our Heart. The message beating in our hearts varies according to the emotions we feel. The energy of the beating, and the field it creates, is what connects to energy currents at a similar vibrational level.

To put it another way, it's as if by focusing on a thought or emotion of any type you were sending a signal to your life that that is what you wish to experience. Indeed, as incredible as it may sound, your thoughts and emotions are genuine orders that you are constantly making to your life (to your Co-Creating Power), whether you're conscious of it or not.

Whatever you focus your attention on, you allow, untie, or create. Therefore, if you focus on something negative, the energy field will offer you new experiences that accord with that emotion. You will have ordered it yourself, albeit without realizing it. This is where it is so vital that you return to your Heart, reassess things from Its perspective, and calm and soothe your ego by focusing on new, more positive thoughts.

The Relief Granted by Space and Time

Fortunately for us we live on a planet of time and space, and, in general, things do not materialize instantaneously. If you've thought badly of something, of yourself or of someone else, that temporal lapse is what will allow you to refocus on your Light and avoid the consequences of your negative thoughts.

Imagine for a moment that this lapse of time didn't exist and every negative thing that you thought materialized instantly in your life. Think about it. Realize that if this is how things were, humanity would have destroyed itself entirely a long time ago. Creation is wise, and having endowed us with an ego, it also gave us the possibility of refocusing our Light at every juncture. It gives us a free will, I, who has the power to choose within you.

Light is infinitely powerful in you. Light is the Essence, and I is the power to act. A single lucid thought can erase a number of dark thoughts that you've had. Only when you spend a lot of time and dedicate much of your attention to dark thoughts will you see the painful consequence of these choices irremediably reflected in your experience.

The good news is that you have the conscious Power to plug yourself into the current of your choice. You and only you can choose, in each moment, to change direction; in other words, to change the level of vibration.

To think, to feel, and to choose are three verbs that only you can conjugate in your life.

CHAPTER 4

You Are Both Light and Darkness, and That Is Fine

The individual cannot equal the perfection of the core that inhabits him, no matter how hard he may try to achieve it.

In society, there is a socio-religious intelligentsia that claims that people should be as perfect as the Being (frequently referred to as the Soul) that inhabits them. However, they forget that not even the Being is perfect, because its nature is twofold, both Light and darkness. Only its core is perfect. Indeed, its core is the perfect co-creator of Light that will expand as it passes through darkness that surrounds it.

REMEMBER: We are innate alchemists!

From childhood, our education, which is itself immersed in a collective forgetting, tells us that we have to change; that we have to be "perfect," to be "good"; that we shouldn't have bad thoughts or bad feelings, even as we are taught to cultivate them; and an endless litany of unattainable demands.

From childhood, we enter into a dichotomy with ourselves in trying to reach objectives that are in themselves unattainable. The person cannot be perfect according to the criteria set by human education. This exigency is born of a nonsense and a contradiction.

We are Beings that evolve through a multitude of experiences in the more or less dense matter that inhabits the Universe. Perfection (Light) does not need to evolve. Expanding It is your only duty. Only the I has the power to choose to expand it, through (using) its body.

We Are Light Crossing Darkness

As mentioned earlier, as a human being, you possess a luminous side and a dark side. The luminous side made a promise to illuminate the dark side that you are passing through. It does this thanks to you, the person who incarnates. No matter how much you try to combat this dark side, you will not make it disappear. It is there and is part of you.

Accept it! Your sole duty is to infuse it with Light, reflecting the innate alchemist that you are.

Through your awakened Heart, you will feel yourself living instead of surviving, flowing with the Purpose of your life. You are the alchemist of your own experience!

Remember that it is by increasing your Light that your Being is able to expand itself! If this were not the case, you simply would not exist in this dark Universe, nor would you inhabit this planet with your human body. So when you look at yourself in the mirror, if you see a human body reflected, it means that inside you there is a Being with its core of Light more or less surrounded by darkness, and that you are certainly endowed with a Heart, which beats and yearns to be awakened, if it isn't already. And yes, that's alright!

And remember, too, that you are the offspring of the All-Creating Love, and though the human being that you have temporarily become may have forgotten the true meaning of its life, He, the Creator, does know what he is doing. For a reason that only belongs to Essence, you exist in order to spread its Light as you pass through a darkness—a darkness with which you will either identify or through which you will heal. That is alchemy!

You Don't Have to Change, Just Change Direction

The messages that assail us from the outside tell us that we must change, but actually, what is it that we must change? Perhaps it is not a question of changing ourselves, in the sense of stopping being imperfect, but rather, changing direction; that is to say, choosing the paths that invariably lead to Yourself (the droplet of the Essence). It is about taking steps that spring from Light, thereby bringing the greatest possible clarity to your path.

It is not necessary to change, only to make the most suitable changes for you!

Stop Fighting Against Yourself

People spend years engaged in an uncontrollable battle against what they don't like about themselves, attempting to change themselves ("I would like to be... "). They don't like —sometimes even can't stand— themselves. They end up believing that to despise, criticize, or punish themselves is the only and best thing they can do. However, what could cause more darkness than mistreating or fighting against yourself? It is not about fighting against anyone or anything with contempt and violence (tricks of the ego).

We may decide we wish to change, but the moment we do so, instead of making the appropriate changes that will allow us to feel better and more at ease with ourselves, we feel flawed. We put in doubt the Perfection of Creation that we partly are, and that has the power to help us feel happy. We are telling the Creating Essence (God, the Creating Parents, or however you wish to refer to it) that what It has created isn't good, isn't enough, or that this part doesn't even exist! We are negating its infinite Heart and its infinite Goodness.

The only possible path to evolution begins with us accepting our perfect nature, which experiences itself in duality, and from there, through conscious choice, in every given moment, to live from our Light.

Accept Your Dual Nature

When we forget our luminous and eternal Reality, we position ourselves in darkness—the very darkness we are experiencing by crossing it. In this oblivious state, we feel lost in dark space, and this leads us to believe that if God has abandoned us in that space-time darkness, so far from Him, it is because we are "bad," so we feel guilty.

Are we?

Not knowing how to answer this intrinsic and unconscious question, we simply fail to trust our own nature. It is then, in a desperate trial to stop feeling so guilty, we subject ourselves instead to the external and socially acceptable criteria. Guilt, an offspring of darkness, is one of the biggest obstacles you can create and place in the way of your Happiness. By going against yourself, you become something like a cloud forming in front of the sun, your own Light.

When we feel guilty, in our obliviousness, we unconsciously punish ourselves for not being good enough; we sabotage and prevent ourselves from truly enjoying our innate well-being, all the while feeling victims of people and circumstances.

Be aware that guilt always seeks punishment. But as suggested by Love, acceptance of our human condition and our duality frees and multiplies higher vibrations, which are charged with Happiness and multiple expressions of Light! Yes, you are a human being, and that condition implies, if you have also forgotten Who You are, that you feel abandoned and guilty.

Does This Mean That Any Bad Thought or Act Is Justified?

No, of course not! Although it is true that you have a dark side (in reality, you are only responsible for that darkness while you are going through it), it is also true that you have (Are) a Heart.

It's not so much question of never having bad feelings or thoughts, but rather, what you choose to do with them once they arise. Those dark feelings and thoughts will arise, whether you like it or not, and whether you accept it or not; they are expressions of the ego that make up your personhood in its totality. That is how it is, and it's okay. Why? Because the only thing that matters is what you decide to do with them.

REMEMBER: In your chest beats a heart, and your Heart is your main creating Tool. You (I) are the artist; you hold the Power to act. The moment a bad thought appears at our conscious level, we have the option of falling with it, bringing it to life and suffering from it, or the power to change it and transform it.

The function of the ego is precisely that, to be egoistic! It proposes ideas, thoughts, emotions, and so forth, but you are the one who, from your Heart, holds the reins.

Reject Punishment

For generations, we have punished ourselves, and have been punished, for having negative thoughts or feelings, believing that we should never think or feel this way—suffering that could be avoided with the simple acceptance of our dual nature.

Can you now see the enormous liberation that comes through something as simple as accepting that it's okay not to be perfect as a person, that the only thing that truly matters for your earthly experience called evolution are your daily decisions?

Don't forget that your natural (dual) imperfection is the engine of your Growth as an expansion of your Light.

The experience that we call evolution will be necessary as long as you do not know and accept yourself sincerely and entirely.

What a marvelous lesson about Love to teach our children!

To accept that you have an ego does not mean that you draw your behavior from it, but simply that you confront it. The ego needs you to educate it as if it were a mischievous and frightened child; sometimes even as if it were a fierce animal that needs to be trained.

Your mission in this life, as in all your past and future lives (experiences), is to contribute with your Love, raise its voice, awaken its echo, and release its vibration, expanding your own luminous core in the process.

Now you may be asking yourself, "Yes, but how do I go about doing this?"

Simple. Just by choosing it!

REMEMBER: You are a constant choice, you are the "I" in the center of the duality that characterizes you, now, along this human life.

Recognize your Light and use it.

Continue reading, and rejoice to discover that this powerful free will is You, namely your I. It is You who decides on Whom and on what you focus your attention: the ego or the Heart. Our ego takes over our minds and all our senses only when we let it.

CHAPTER 5

The Trinity in You

The only way to evolve is to choose, at each moment,
to heed the voice of your Heart.

How marvelous is this game called Life. Doesn't it seem marvelous to you to be unconditionally and naturally endowed with the Power to choose, at each moment, the role that you wish to play on this planet, in this small creation? Life as you know it now (Eternal Walk) offers you the total freedom to discover your own paths and to fully enjoy everything that you can possibly desire today.

Once incarnated in your physical body—an offspring of matter and therefore of slow vibration—your Being manifests itself in your person in three well-defined aspects: your ego (darkness), your I (free will), and your Heart (cradle of your Essence, Love). These three parts will allow you to evolve as I, thanks to your continuous choices and experiences. The more attention given to your Heart, the more you grow.

The Essence in you does not need to evolve because It Is the divine droplet in you. The darkness is not yours; you are only passing through it.

Your Heart

Your Heart holds your luminous core, your perfect Being. It is the Love in you, the most luminous and powerful Tool in you, unconditionally at your disposal. It is symbolically located in the center of your chest.

Your Heart shelters the luminous Essence in you. Do you remember that droplet, which was released from the Absolute? To return there is to always get back in touch with your Creating Parents of Love. Those Parents are the ones who always love you and are there for you, who created you from their infinite Love, so that day by day you too could choose to transform yourself into their own manifestation.

Choose to become a co-creator of Love, and let Happiness flow through your life like the blood courses through your veins.

It is no coincidence that throughout the annals of history and the rich tapestry of cultures, human beings have identified Love with a heart and have placed the emotion of Love in the center of the chest. Just as your heart (the organ) distributes blood to your entire body, if you choose to use it daily, your Heart (energetic, vibrating) distributes and re-creates Joy throughout your life.

Your I

Your I is the cradle of your freedom, your expression. It is the passenger in your taxi. Your I is your free will, your possibility of choosing, in each moment, between either Love and its multiple expressions—peace, well-being, kindness, and wealth—or the relentless nightmares that your ego seeks to impose on you. Symbolically, we locate the I in the solar plexus.

Your I, located between the two states that make you a person, Light and darkness, is the inner voice that expresses your choice.

Your awakened I, alert to your Heart and in harmonious communication with the driver in you (the mind), will be who decides, in each moment, to cross the paths of the ego (darkness) from within the Peace of your Heart (Light). On the other hand, your dormant I, confused by your ego, when crossing the path of darkness will lose itself in it, experiencing and suffering its ever-painful consequences.

In you, your I is that which speaks with your Heart, your ego, and your physical body. It is that which elects, by means of your body, to bring forth and share the Light or the darkness through your thoughts, emotions, decisions, feelings, relationships, and actions. In each moment, it can elect to become the co-creating prince of the Heart of Existence or the soldier of darkness.

Your Ego

Your ego symbolizes the dark space that your Being and your whole person, crosses. Its function is to destroy, to provoke your Essence. In fact, it only seeks to be illuminated by the Light of your powerful Heart—exactly like a child who misbehaves in a search for limits that will allow him to feel safe and at peace.

The Ego Is Your Best Ally

Your ego is continually proposing dark thoughts, feelings, ideas, and actions to you so that you, from your I, can choose what to do with them—to heed them, thereby allowing them to materialize in your path, or to choose to immediately plug into the luminous presence of your Heart.

The ego, which for centuries was harshly criticized and rejected, is, in reality, our greatest ally. Although from a rational standpoint it may seem paradoxical, your ego proposes dark thoughts and emotions with the sole intention of having you reject them, because once you do, you set your ego free. Yes, your ego simply wants you to Heal it; to perform your duty as alchemist. It is only when you don't—when you choose not to heed the voice of Love—that your ego punishes you.

Picture a young executive who has an interview for a marvelous job that he has always desired. He has been sending out resumes for months, and finally they've agreed to interview him. He's waiting his turn, alongside other candidates in an elegant waiting room, when his ego begins to taunt him.

"Look at how many people there are; there's sure to be someone more qualified than you. You're not going to get the job…"

The candidate starts getting nervous. He sees an attractive and classy girl waiting her turn. The voice of his ego seizes the opportunity and takes it a step farther.

"She's going to get the job. They always give it to good-looking people. It makes no difference what you studied; with your horrible nose you're not going to get anywhere. Who would want to see that ugly nose every day?"

His insecurity increases as swiftly as his self-esteem plummets. He feels a knot in his stomach and starts to sweat. His ego, now feeling stronger and more important, gains momentum.

"You might as well leave. I don't know why you're wasting your time. You're starting to look ridiculous. You should have stayed in bed this morning."

Increasingly nervous and powerless with each passing moment, his hands start to sweat, his pulse quickens, and he feels as if his heart is about to burst. His ego takes advantage of his weakness to go even farther.

"Actually, why do you even want this job? You're not up to the task, and everyone is going to know it. You're going to have to change careers, find something that you're capable of doing, something easier, more on your level, even if that means earning less and working more. In the end, who really cares?"

The door of the main office begins to open and the afflicted candidate listens to the self-assured voice of another candidate coming out.

His ego insists, "You're pathetic. Everyone is laughing at you. You're clumsy, and everyone sees it."

The door opens wider, and an elegant executive looks at him, gesturing for him to enter. The aspiring executive stands up, feeling wretched. His legs quiver, and he gets a little dizzy. What do you think the outcome of this interview will be?

This young man has gone from vibrant enthusiasm at the prospect of a fantastic job to utter insecurity and nervousness, dragged down to weakness and a total lack of confidence by his ego in a matter of minutes. By listening to the voice of darkness, this young man has conceded his power to his ego. The alchemy has not occurred.

The consequences of giving too much importance to our egos can be devastating. In the case of this young man it ruined his interview, but for you, it could just as well be other and no less vital things in life: bad relationships, problems with your partner, economic problems, work problems, health problems, sadness, anxiety, and so on.

Actually, the young man's ego simply longed to be quieted down from the very outset. The ego is frightened and needs your support and security. It needs to be healed with the Loving clarifications of your Heart.

It is at the moment in which the person listens to the ego and bestows power on it, that the ego becomes desperate, rebels, and attacks the body and all its functions. Its task is not to harm us, but to offer us a reason and opportunity to transform it. From the moment we fail to choose the path of Love, the ego increases its presence, making us feel miserable.

How differently things might have turned out if prior to the incursions by the ego, the young man had firmly quieted it down from the Peace in his Heart; if instead of listening to his ego, he had freely chosen, with the aid of his I, to center himself in his luminous Heart; if he had said to his ego something like, "Shhh, this is none of your business. I'll take care of this. This job is mine. I'm more than prepared for it, and I'm the perfect candidate for it."

If he had done all of those things, he would have felt at peace and from there, more serene and secure. Perhaps the ego would have continued its assault somewhat, but it could not have had the same effect on someone paying attention to his confidence levels. And finally, the little dark voice in him would have been quelled, bringing the interview to a very different and satisfactory conclusion. Recover your Power!

REMEMBER: Power only resides in the Heart.

Put Your Ego at Ease

The habit of quieting down the ego is acquired through affection for oneself and daily practice. The ego, accustomed to us listening and relinquishing all our functions and senses to it—and therefore all our Power—gets scared when we start to quiet it down. We cannot simply ignore it and pretend it's not there. It is there; it exists, and in this earthly experience it is a part of you! Continuing to ignore it by choosing not to realize that the more you use it the more it imposes itself will make you feel lost and completely miserable, dizzy, and affected by a whirlwind of dark emotions.

In the following chapters, I will show you how to kindly but firmly quiet down and soothe your ego just as you would a small child.

Listening to Your Ego: Habit or Exception?

Think for a moment about this Universe in which we live. What predominates: light or darkness? If you look at photographs taken by NASA, you will see that this Universe is predominantly dark. In fact, if you observe closely, it is indeed very dark, barely illuminated by tiny lights here and there.

The human mind, in order to survive, created the concepts of night and day to avoid the fact that what we call darkness is the only Reality of our planet: we are floating in an immense darkness. The light of the sun during what we call "daytime" offers us respite, created by and for the mind in order to help us survive. Daytime is a reality constructed by our mind; we have made of night a transition required for us to sleep.

Given that this is the only Universe that we know, it escapes our reason to consider the possibility that there are other universes in which light prevails over darkness, where, unlike here, the brilliantly colored light that engulfs everything is interrupted solely by small flecks of darkness floating in the distance and in isolation. Nevertheless, that is the way it is. These universes exist and are waiting for us to choose them.

As a Being, you have elected to temporarily live in this dark Universe with the sole purpose of offering it your Loving, Joyful, Rich, and Ingenious Heart along your path; in other words, to offer your Love to your feeling of abandonment. You have understood that, as a human being, the only way to heal this darkness you are temporarily crossing is for the I in you to choose to write your story from the Love that nurtures your Heart. Each time you do so, your core expands and decreases a little bit more the darkness of this Universe that you now inhabit.

The Love inside you is the Light, unique on your path.

It is not surprising that in a Universe in which darkness predominates, it is easier to plug ourselves into and remain within our egos instead of our Hearts. We could say that the automatic response of the human is to listen to the voice of his ego. It requires Love, continuous attention, and the resolution of being mindful of our inner selves to remain in our Light. Nevertheless, when we realize that the reward will invariably be Happiness and success in all its forms, we will no longer doubt the value of being mindful. And if, in addition to this, we realize that our Happiness has consequences that reach far beyond our little human lives, helping to lessen the suffering of this and other worlds, the decision is that much clearer.

I am the light in my path and in my path nothing is more important than I!

Let's look at another example of how our ego works. Imagine two friends having an argument. One of them reproaches the other for having forgotten her birthday. The other gets instantly defensive and insists that she *did* call her but the other didn't pick up the phone.

Each one is convinced of her position and tries to persuade the other that their version is the only true and valid one. Clinging to their rigid thoughts, the tension heightens, their heart rates go up, and they feel miserable: one gets a sore neck and a headache, while the other feels a knot in her stomach.

Both of them feel angry, sad, frustrated, and misunderstood. Imprisoned by their own darkness, the emotions they feel are translated into physical discomfort. The two friends are relinquishing their power to their egos, something that inevitably has negative consequences, both physically and emotionally. Their egos are punishing them for having materialized darkness instead of transforming it. This discomfort is the manner in which their Being lets them know that what they are doing or thinking is not good for them and their evolution; that it tarnishes the Light in their Hearts.

Every physical discomfort or emotional suffering that we face in the course of our lives is a signal or warning issued by our Being to urge us to change our behaviors with Love. If we fail in this, we shirk our responsibility to love and enliven the path that we chose before our present incarnation. Pay attention to your own signals. Any time you feel the least bit of fear, painful emotion, unpleasant sensation, or any type of physical discomfort, ask yourself what your Being is trying to tell you or what you may be doing or failing to do that goes against your own Happiness.

Let's return to the two friends. Imagine that, at a certain point in the argument, one of them chose to pay attention to her Heart. She might think something like: "Actually, what's the big deal? I don't want us to be angry at each other. I care for her very much, and know that she cares for me. And if right now she has trouble acknowledging that she forgot my birthday, she may do it later on."

Just this lucid change in the woman's thinking will trigger an immediate sense of relief, thus quieting the ego in its attempt to darken the loving relationship between the two friends. This is alchemy! The luminous vibrational wave emitted by that more loving and understanding behavior creates a sense of relief and will be perceived by her friend's energy body, no matter how angry she may be.

Following the argument, both of them will have felt a great burden lifted from their shoulders. Many people with whom I work describe their feelings following a quarrel as one of physical exhaustion, and some compare it to having run a marathon.

REMEMBER: Contrary to what we have always believed, darkness is not the enemy; it is what we do when we are in it and what we do with it that is dangerous. It is when we pass through it using our ego that the danger arises.

Choose Your Heart!

Jodie is a woman in her thirties who came to see me because she had been in the throes of depression for several months, a depression that she despaired of finding a way out of. After having attended one of my conferences, she had felt something release inside and was able to leave her house and visit me for a session. In that first session, Jodie told me how, in her view, the breakup with a man was the cause of her feeling so miserable. In the course of the meeting she realized that, following the split, she had started listening and giving importance exclusively to the voice of her ego. Her ego relentlessly repeated that she would never be able to find someone who would truly love her. To make matters worse, her unruly ego kept saying that if she didn't live with a man, she, as a woman, wouldn't be capable of supporting herself in life. Jodie, paying attention to and nearly obsessed by her ego's messages, felt worse and worse, more hopeless and exhausted with each passing day. Little by little, she had stopped wanting to go out, and ended up so physically drained that she would spend days lying in bed or on the sofa.

As a result of paying sole attention to her ego, Jodie had become trapped in a vicious cycle which, for a long time, she felt she couldn't escape from. I accompanied her so that she could learn to listen to the voice of her Heart and identify the voice of her ego in order to be able to soothe it kindly but firmly. As she gradually regained her power, taking importance away from her ego, she began to feel freer, more vibrant, and joyful. Three months and four sessions later, Jodie had recovered and decided to start her own business. Freed of the constant influence of her ego, her business quickly flourished. A year later she began to share her life with the man who, to this day, is her partner.

REMEMBER: Darkness *does* want you to pay attention to it, but only by using your Heart.

Become the alchemist of your own Life: evolve as a person from your Peace.

CHAPTER 6

The Promises You Made
Before You Were Born

Do you remember the two promises you, as a Being, made to yourself before inhabiting this body? Don't worry, you're not alone. If you're like 99.9 percent of the world's population, you will simply have forgotten them. The answer, however, as always, lies within.

Allow yourself to re-establish contact with your Being. Begin once more to listen to its voice which, from its Essence, is pure Love and Knowledge, and you too will naturally and easily remember everything that you promised yourself before your incarnation.

REMEMBER: There is nothing that I can do or see that you cannot equally do or see.

In the following chapters, I will show you a technique called "centering" that will allow you to regain this forgotten contact to yourself, to your Being, to your own Love and Knowledge, with that Happiness that this contact brings to you and expands in you.

FIRST PROMISE: You Promised Yourself to Continue Loving and Illuminating Your Darkness by Pursuing Your Mission.

Prior to being born, you chose a unique mission. That mission is the way in which you intended to carry on with your Purpose, the transformation of your darkness into Light during this earthly life.

If your ultimate aim, your Purpose, is to continue evolving—expanding your Love—in this earthly experience by means of your decisions, behaviors, emotions, and relationships, then your mission is the way you chose to express this Purpose in this life. For some it might be through an art, for others conveying a message, for still others being an example of affection, courage, creativity, and so on.

Having forgotten, just like the taxi driver, that you are carrying a passenger, namely your Being, and that your sole reason for existence as a person is to manifest it, you will have also forgotten to fulfill your promise. You will even have forgotten what your mission is. It's okay! You simply were mistaken. What joy it is to be able to remember and resume your path in the eternal present!

It doesn't matter how much time you've spent mistakenly and unconsciously neglecting your Heart and promoting your darkness, nor does it matter how much you've increased it. You have the irrevocable Power to choose, here and now, to enhance the Love in your experience. It doesn't matter if you've spent twenty or eighty years in oblivion; you have the Power to enhance your Light now, in the present moment. You just have to choose to do so.

Ask yourself this: What are eighty earthly years compared to the eternity of your existence? The years in this life that you may have spent in oblivion lose all their gravity the moment you are conscious of this reality and decide to forgive yourself.

Your Parents, the Creating Essence in you, love you unconditionally. They do not judge you; they love you no matter what you do. They have no need to forgive you for your mistakes; they love you plain and simple. Love does not require forgiveness. Love is forgiveness, compassion, and understanding. Your Parents love you; they never get tired of waiting for you. So, do you dare to forgive and love yourself?

SECOND PROMISE: You Promised Yourself Not to Repeat the Negative Behaviors That You Had Already Experienced in Other Lives.

As a result of the infinite number of experiences which, as a Being, you have already known, you have already used a series of negative behaviors, tendencies, and attitudes. Before your incarnation, you decided no longer to behave according to the darkness you had already experienced in other lives. You promised yourself not to repeat the misguided behaviors that have always been so painful for you.

The vital choices that each Being makes to facilitate the fulfillment of this promise utterly elude the human mind's comprehension. In order not to revert to the negative behaviors of its past, the Being will choose a place of birth, type of physical parents, physical features, health predispositions, and all manner of circumstances in order to fulfill its promise.

What to our limited, critical, and ever-judgmental human mind may seem horrible, such as a baby being born into an abusive family in a country where misery, atrocity, hunger, and poverty are rampant, in reality is nothing other than the choice of that individual's Being before its incarnation. Remember that although the human mind only perceives the tender and tiny body of a defenseless baby, in reality, it is simply the vehicle chosen by a Being that has had centuries, if not millennia, of life and experience. Disconnected as we are from our Knowledge, we see only an innocent and defenseless baby, and we forget that the Being that inhabits had its own powerful reasons for choosing that particular vital experience.

The creating Essence in all of us is Wisdom, Serenity and Knowledge itself; therefore, would you doubt and believe that this Light in all of us could have made an error? Only from the arrogance of the ignorant human mind could we arrive at this conclusion. Yes, I know it isn't easy to witness the horror and suffering that many Beings decide to live through on this planet, but of course, neither I, nor you, nor anybody else can judge these decisions. The only thing you can do in an environment where there is suffering is to show and offer your unconditional Love and support and, if you can, support those who ask for it.

Imagine that someone had been an abuser in another life. Perhaps he would choose to be born into a social and family situation that would remind him not to repeat the kind of behavior he had already used. He may choose to suffer the consequences of that type of abuse himself, or be born into a country at war or into a persecuted or marginalized social group. Suffering the consequences of that past behavior himself, he will always remember not to repeat it.

A person who generally used aggression in other lives may choose an environment that will remind him no longer to use it. It is possible that he may choose biological parents who themselves use aggression, or choose a place where people are generally aggressive or where violent conflicts occur.

A person who was sad and submissive in other lives will choose situations, people, and places that remind her of that behavior, so that she is mindful of the fact that it is not what she wants in this life. She may choose a progenitor that herself subjects her husband to this kind of treatment, or on the contrary, a progenitor that is himself constantly submissive and sad. She may choose to be born into a social group that is particularly submissive or that suffers from a sense of collective injustice or powerlessness.

A Being that had a past life that was monotonous or boring may choose to be born into an environment that reminds it of its cowardice and incites it to be courageous, such as being born in a remote village in the country where there are hardly any possibilities for contact with others and having at the same time an ardent wish to be a singer. Or, as another example, this Being may choose to be born a woman passionate about law in a conservative family where, traditionally, women don't work.

A Being that had suffered from emotional dependency, depending on others for its emotional well-being, might choose an environment where someone is completely dependent on it. In this way, it will remember how damaging its own behavior was and will remember not to repeat it.

Let me point out that if a Being chooses a vital experience that is harsh, difficult, or even atrocious to your eyes, it does not directly correlate with the degree of darkness that it experienced in past lives. The life of Hitler, it seems, was no more difficult than a boy who is born with a painful brain tumor, although the darkness that Hitler brought with him into the world was probably greater. If there is a golden rule that you can always follow, it is never to judge others under any circumstances. Don't try to guess if this or that Being is or isn't dark due to the experiences that it has chosen to pursue in this life. This is as absurd as trying to find out if someone uses their Heart according to whether he is good-looking or not. Turn your back on judgment and criticism; cast them aside, and simply observe things from within the inexhaustible goodness of your Heart.

REMEMBER: The time you spend paying attention to others is time taken away from your own evolution.

And what about you? Do you remember what kind of behavior you promised yourself to leave behind? I'll give you a hint: Just look at the negative behaviors displayed by your biological parents to clearly see which behaviors you decided not to reuse.

Your Biological Parents Are Your Masters In What Not to Do, and In What Behaviors You Can't Repeat

The moment in which as a Being you decided to be incarnated, you already knew that of all the people you were going to live with in this incarnation, your biological parents would be the ones who could most easily reflect your old modes of behavior, which you promised yourself not to use any more.

Indeed, as surprising as it may sound, you chose your physical parents to remind you what not to do. You chose them as your best allies, as the only acceptable external teachers for your evolution.

NOTE: Henceforth, to avoid confusion I will use the term "Parents" capitalized to refer to your Essential Parents and the lower-case form of parents to refer to your biological parents.

Part Two

Be Grateful To
Your Parents

You Chose Your Parents in Order to Remember What Not to Do

As a Being, you were aware of what the two human beings who were going to become your earthly parents were like, so before you were born you chose that man and that woman—whom today you call Mom and Dad—to become the "manufacturers" of your physical body. These biological parents are merely reproducers of something that had been created previously, but in no way does that make them Creators of Life.

Then why do we bestow the title of "Parents" on our biological parents? The biological parents whom we erroneously call "Parents" are the manufacturers of our vehicle; they have simply reproduced us, whereas it is the Essential Father and Mother in us who have created and conceived us.

Whether or not we acknowledge it, we are the eternal and beloved children of the unconditional Creating Love. To give you an example, think of a light bulb. It is manufactured by machines operated and controlled by workers in a factory. Wouldn't it be unthinkable to consider these machines or those that control them the creators or the inventors of the light bulb?

Your Biological Parents Serve as an Example of What Not to Do

You chose your parents with a single purpose: that they would serve as an example of what not to do. Yes, you can reread that sentence to make sure you've understood it.

I said, as an example of what *not* to do. The good in them, just like the good in you, comes from the Infinite Love, from the Creative Essence.

Why did you choose those manufacturers above all others?

Simply because, of all their behaviors, the dark ones are precisely those that you yourself, prior to being born, chose not to repeat. Seeing them reflected in your parents' daily behavior, you would be mindful of them and thus easily remember what it is that you promised yourself not to manifest again.

When dealing with this subject in my sessions or conferences, I often find myself faced with people who feel liberated when they realize that Mom and Dad are not gods or goddesses that they have to bow down to, and that they do not have to judge or hate either of them. They are simply human beings that, under the gaze of God, Father-Mother, become brothers and sisters. But let's keep talking about them as your biological parents on this planet.

Just like all human beings who inhabit this planet, your mom and dad also are an infinitely Loving core that has detached itself from the Essential Source of Love to travel through the immensely spacious darkness. Therefore, through their comings and goings and throughout their experiences in this space, they also have a series of more or less dark and negative behaviors just like all of us, and that's okay.

What is most important to you as their "child" is to be able to see them as they are, with their defects and virtues. Only then, from this lucid and loving perspective, will you be able to love them freely and honestly, or at least respect them if your relationship with them has been hard or difficult.

And What About Their Good Behaviors?

Like some of my students, you may be asking yourself, "What about the other aspects of their behavior, the good ones? Should I not emulate them in this respect?"

We have clearly not copied these loving behaviors from humans. They arise from the creating Essence itself throughout our experiences.

It's like a cherry tree in spring, which, after having delighted us with its beautiful flowers and having fattened up its succulent and fragrant cherries, finally lets fall its fruits. One of the fallen cherries germinates. Little by little, it grows into a cherry tree which, in turn, brings forth more flowers and delicious cherries. Would you say that it bears fruit and flowers because it imitated its father tree, or rather that the Source itself has created and endowed it with the capacity to bear fruit? Just as the cherry tree does not need to imitate its father tree to blossom and yield fruit, we do not need to imitate any external behavior to let the Light and Love that resides in us shine forth.

You, Too, Were Intended to Be Their Master

Before being incarnated, given your already infinite compassion and affection for these two people who were to be your biological parents, you also promised to be an example of Love to them. In contrast with those negative behaviors, which they not only used but were going to teach you to use, through your own behaviors you intended to show them—without the need for lectures—that there were other options, that choosing the Love present in their Hearts would be a valid option that would doubtless also be good for them and completely within their reach.

Aidan was eighteen years old when he came to see me on the advice of his father, a wealthy attorney from Los Angeles who had taken part in one of my conferences. For a few months, the young man had been suffering from panic attacks that were gradually leading him into total seclusion. The unfortunate emotional state in which he found himself was seriously affecting his studies. His father was worried that if he didn't recover soon he would lose his place at Yale.

A few minutes into the session, Aidan told me that he was embarking on a career in law in a continuation of a family tradition that spanned seven generations of male lawyers. However, he hated the prospect. Acting was his real and only passion.

Aidan felt himself caught between a rock and a hard place. On the one hand, he did not want to disappoint his father, especially since his mother had just died; on the other hand, he didn't want to abandon his dream of performing on stage.

After a few sessions, Aidan resolved to speak with his still intransigent father. The honest and affectionate young man explained to his father how he felt and told him that he had decided to discontinue his law career and had applied to a dramatic arts school.

Initially, the father fought tooth and nail for his only son's resumption of his law studies; however, a few months later, seeing how happy his son was, and how well he had recovered, he came to thank me personally. With tears of joy in his eyes, he told me how much he admired his son for daring to pursue what he himself had not had the courage to do in his own youth.

Yes, you, too, chose to become a master to your biological parents, but, do you remember what you promised yourself to teach them? I could give you numerous instances of how my students, by making beneficial changes in their lives, gradually become the masters and examples they promised to be for their parents. One such instance is that of Martha.

Martha was a middle-aged woman who came to see me because she wanted to increase her income and gain financial security. Martha told me that her mother was a submissive and fearful woman who, having lost her husband, quickly married another man. In spite of the aggressive and unpleasant nature of her new husband, he provided her with a luxurious home and ensured that she herself did not have to work. Martha could not stand to see what her mother had become, and after a heated argument on the phone, they had stopped all communication. This had happened a year previously.

In our first session, the young woman soon realized that until then, it was she who, imitating her mother's behavior, had not allowed herself to have any professional success or financial independence. Paradoxically, while criticizing her mother's actions, she had also failed to break this dark pattern in which both of them were trapped.

A few months later, when Martha landed a well-paid job that she had not even allowed herself to dream about before and that also allowed her to spend more time at home with her family, she decided to contact her mother.

Only a few months were enough for the once submissive mother to also begin to see her life differently. She gave her husband an ultimatum: Either he would start treating her better, or she would leave him. To everyone's surprise, the husband, devastated by the prospect of losing his wife, enlisted my help to break the pattern of behavior that he was in and that was about to ruin his marriage. He, like many others, was imitating the behaviors learned and copied from his own biological parents. In the end, however, his Heart prevailed over his ego.

The Great Contradiction of Our Lives

If we choose our biological parents in order to remind us, through their daily and darkest behaviors, what not to do, at the same time being an example to them of what *to* do, isn't it surprising that we do the exact opposite? How many people do you know who do not imitate their biological parents precisely in their negative behavior, about which, moreover, they complain?

This is where the real contradiction of our entire lives is rooted. How can we love or feel happy when we are turning our backs on ourselves, when we are blind to the promise we made to ourselves, and that we have abandoned: the affection or at least the compassion that we already felt for our future masters, our mom and dad?

In light of this, doesn't it seem a genuine contradiction to continuously criticize them, accuse them, or even hate them?

We all go through teenage years when it becomes clear that Mom and Dad are not the gods we had blindly trusted ever since we were born. However, it is necessary to leave this tumultuous period to first reconcile with yourself and accept that it has been you who has been mistaken about these "gods," and that they have only done the best they could and knew how to do.

It is yourself with whom you need to make peace; only then will you be able to heal all your relationships. You chose them in the full knowledge that they could help you! They were to be your daily masters!

Perhaps if you are someone who has suffered through a difficult or traumatic childhood, you might feel affronted by what I'm saying. Maybe you think that you have a legitimate reason to hate them. Maybe you are like some of my students who, initially, reject the prospect of forgiving their parents because they hold them solely responsible for their suffering, misfortune, and their entire miserable lives.

I know it's not easy growing up with tyrannical or abusive parents, but I can also tell you that, as difficult as your experience with them may have been or may be, you, as a Being, already knew them before choosing them. You chose them in the full knowledge of what they were like and what you wanted to learn from your relationship with them. Perhaps, until now, overwhelmed as you are in your pain, you haven't seen this, and you've refused the possibility of evolving by forgiving and continuing on your path as a free human being.

REMEMBER: Nobody is judging you! Your true Parents, the Creating Love, love you and will always do so unconditionally, whatever you do. Looking at you with their infinite Love and Compassion, they see that you have simply forgotten Them and thus have become a prisoner of your errors and your suffering.

The Great Confusion

Society, religion, popular culture, and family culture encourage you to resemble someone external to yourself. First your mom and dad, then your extended family, the members of your social group, the inhabitants of your country, and so on.

"Like breeds like." "The apple does not fall far from the tree." Do these expressions ring a bell? The message they teach us throughout our education is the same across all continents, races, and cultures: Identify with your biological parents, and thereby, forget your Eternal Parents.

By identifying with our biological parents, we forget Who we are and what we came to do in this earthly experience. Having forgotten, and oblivious to the fact that the Creating Essence resides inside us, we bestow on our biological parents a kind of superpower, which in reality belongs to our Eternal Creating Parents.

In a certain sense, we make of them our gods. We mistakenly and dangerously grant them the title of Creators. Instead of seeing them as having the defects and weaknesses that are intrinsic to the human race and accepting them as such, we demand from them all kinds of behaviors and create expectations which, try as they might, they could never fulfill. We forget that they, too, like us, have forgotten who they are.

Misunderstood Adolescence

As we grow up, we discover that those we call our parents, our biological parents, do not have all the answers, that they cannot alleviate our suffering nor prevent death, and thus we feel profoundly disillusioned. As a result of forgetting Who we are, we feel alone in the face of the danger of Life.

It is in adolescence that we begin to realize that these gods are not what they seem. We feel let down and blame them. We feel anger, but at the same time we feel guilty for this anger toward those we have deified, thereby creating a vicious cycle of misery that is hard to escape from.

As you may have guessed, this is precisely the root of all so-called "adolescent problems." These adolescents, disconnected from their own luminous core, suddenly feel alone; they feel deceived and disappointed, with no direction, with no hope or aspirations, and with nothing that might fill their profound existential vacuum.

The moment when we reach adulthood should be one of enjoyment and celebration. It is a time of life when our dreams and professional aspirations finally take shape and can be expressed, a time when we can finally manifest our mission to the best of our abilities, and a time that is naturally, although not normally, a moment of joy, enjoyment, and personal fulfillment.

Love or Necessity

As I pointed out before, there are people who never get through the phase of differentiation that adolescence represents and arrive in adulthood with the infantile belief that their biological parents are perfect.

I am sometimes faced with students who, when asked to give three of their parents' flaws, are offended or incensed that I would dare to imply that their parents might have flaws to begin with. Others are simply surprised, given that they have never entertained the notion that their biological parents might have defects of any kind, although some are surprised that I only ask for three.

How can we love someone whom we have idolized? Is it possible to love someone whom we do not see as they really are? Is it them we love, or is it our illusion of who they are and what they're like that we love?

To love implies at least to be lucid enough to see the other as he is; with their flaws and their virtues, which, as human beings, whether we like it or not, we all have.

Do you realize how different the parent-child relationship could be without these false expectations and simultaneous demands by the ego?

CHAPTER 8

How Do You Sabotage Yourself?

*Lost in oblivion and confusion, we act from our egos
to avoid feeling the painful emotions that are born
of our deepest emotional needs.*

On this planet, tireless traveler through our dark Universe, each and every one of us displays a range of dark behaviors and thoughts, more or less destructive, which we use to sabotage our Happiness in everyday life. These behaviors and thoughts are precisely those we promised ourselves we would not display, and are in large measure imitated, learned, and copied from others.

But why do we choose to use these dark forms of copied thinking and acting? What makes us imitate our biological parents precisely in their darkest part? What is it that makes us listen to our egos before we listen to our Hearts?

The moment we forget Who we are, and forget that, like everyone else, we are loved by the Essence that inhabits our inner selves, we begin to seek Love and role models outside of ourselves; we seek to be loved, acknowledged, and to belong to something larger than our bodies; we seek security because we forget that it resides inside us, and this is how we look for the approval and recognition (confusing it with Love) from our biological parents, even at the cost of our true Happiness.

We pretend to be good instead of naturally and sincerely being so.

The fear that arises from our forgetting that we are Children of the Essence leads us to the need that keeps us prisoner—to seek out, by all means, external love, approval, recognition, and acceptance. It is a desperate attempt to win the love and approval of others because we have failed to approve of ourselves. But what mirror can reflect your image with dark hair if you are blond?

Remember that the ego is the voice of the darkness that surrounds your Being, and therefore, comes into this world with its own dark memories of your previous life experiences. Your constant encounters with the darkness in your daily life are such that the ego feels immediately identified with them. It imitates and even learns these negative thoughts and behaviors, which it will then propose to you so that you will manifest them.

Do you remember the example of the two friends arguing? The former will argue to avoid feeling the pain and guilt of knowing that she did something wrong, and the latter will do so to avoid feeling abandoned and unloved by her friend.

These behaviors imprison and oppress the alchemist in you. This lack of acknowledgement when faced with equivocation can only trigger feelings of frustration on the one hand and discomfort and guilt on the other—feelings that our ego incessantly bombards us with, if we have not yet learned how to educate and quiet it.

The painful emotions that our egos know how to arouse so easily have their roots in emotional needs. These are products of the emptiness left behind as a result of having forgotten Who we are. We forget that all the answers lie inside us, as well as kindness, humility, joy, and all the ingredients required to feel happy and fully enjoy this life.

Imagine, for instance, that you are a woman in her thirties who has made a date to have dinner with an attractive person whom you happen to truly like. It's your first date with this person, and you've decided to wear a dress that suits you well and just be yourself. At this point, your ego will most probably begin to taunt you, making you feel like your date is not going to like you enough to risk the solid and stable relationship that you have dreamed of for years. It will tell you that you're getting older and the chances of finding your ideal partner are diminishing. Perhaps it will even say that if you don't get married soon, you'll end up an old maid and that it will be too late to have kids.

Suddenly you feel a rush of nervous emotion and insecurity, which only abates slightly when you decisively go out and buy a splendid new dress that you can't afford and a pair of heels that are as high as they are uncomfortable, which embellish your figure and destroy your spine. The dress cost half a month's rent and the heels are guaranteed to make your feet and back hurt, but you bought them, despite the pain, in order to avoid the painful emotions of anguish, loneliness, and fear of rejection. These uncontrolled thoughts, which your ego has proposed to you and that you have heeded, have no doubt struck upon three basic needs in you: security, control, and approval.

REMEMBER: The Heart does not need; the Heart Is the one who can offer. Needs always belong to the realm of the ego.

Punishment or Reward

All of our negative behaviors are solely focused on avoiding punishment and obtaining reward. From childhood onward, you understood that imitating certain forms of behavior was going to help you get a reward: the affection of your mom and dad; or it was going to help you avoid punishment, which, symbolically, at least, meant the withdrawal of their affection and approval.

As you grow older, you glean these forms of behavior and needs from your surroundings, so that every time you behave from your ego you do it to avoid a painful emotion, such as the anger of friends or society, loss of love, loss of social standing, the disapproval of others, solitude, lack of security, and so on, or to obtain a pleasurable emotion, such as recognition by a group, an attractive partner, being liked by others, being seen and admired, feeling security while knowing that it is false, and so forth.

A human being who maintains harmonious communication with the luminous part of his Being will be mostly free of the needs of his ego. Such a person, attuned to himself, is a person who loves and accepts himself as a whole. He does not ignore his Being; he loves and feels loved and supported by the Essence itself. He doesn't doubt his own greatness, although with complete humility, and therefore does not seek or need the recognition and approval of others.

Is this something you would like for yourself?

The Needs of the Ego

We could spend hours and entire chapters of this book finding and classifying human needs. To make our task easier, however, we will put them in three global categories:

- the need for security;
- the need for control;
- the need for approval.

THE NEED FOR SECURITY: Disconnected from ourselves, we feel fear. We feel insecure and frightened. We view the world as a dangerous place in which we must fight to survive, and we see others as potential enemies. Some of the behaviors that stem from this need include being defensive, attacking, taking revenge, surviving, and being overprotective of oneself and others. Have you ever observed people who are always smothering their kids? It's as if they are obsessed that something bad is going to happen to them, when there is nothing to justify it.

THE NEED FOR CONTROL: Feeling abandoned by creation itself, or simply ignoring its presence within us, we stop trusting our Lives. As a result, we find ourselves needing to control or change people, situations, or things in order to avoid feeling the uncontrollable fear that things will not turn out as we expect them to.

Manipulating, forcing, trying to convince, trying to be "number one" or the best, needing to be right, or wanting things done only your way—does this ring a bell? These are only some of the behaviors we employ to alleviate the need for control of the human ego.

Some examples of this behavior, which we all face at some time or another, include mothers who manipulate their children to behave in the way they think is best, people who play the victim in order to obtain what they want, or people who want their partners to do things their way or constantly need to know where their partners are, with whom, and why at every moment. Taken to an extreme, this is the need behind all forms of fanaticism and intransigence.

THE NEED FOR APPROVAL: The need for approval stems from lack of love for oneself and lack of self-support. Motivated by this need for approval, we seek recognition from others: first from our parents and then in our partners and others.

Some of the behaviors we typically use to sate this need are: seeking acceptance, looking for a pat on the back or general recognition, wanting to be liked, being seductive, and oftentimes, even saying or doing things we don't like to garner approval and appreciation.

Surely you can think of many people who act according to this need: people who pursue studies expected by their parents, go out with the type of person whom their parents consider respectable; people who are constantly being funny or clever, or who, when dressing, choose clothing that will attract and seduce others, rather than wearing something for the comfort, well-being, and health it provides.

Identify the Needs Your Ego Employs

Identifying the emotional needs your ego makes use of will allow you to discover the root causes of your dark behaviors and why you have been continually using these behaviors in your daily life. In this way, you will become aware of what causes the painful emotions you feel everyday. It will allow you to get to know your ego and detect its numerous manipulative ways better, thereby giving you the means to more easily and more quickly deal with thoughts, emotions, or behaviors that are harmful to you.

Observe yourself with Love and acceptance, as you discover which of the following three roles you have developed inside the most until now: the tyrant, the victim, or the ignorant hyper-rational.

And don't worry! You're not alone in this. All of us, as human beings, struggle daily with our egos.

REMEMBER: Residing in and acting from darkness is the norm and not the exception on our planet—until now.

Simply be loving and forgiving with yourself, and continue on your path joyfully! Do not hesitate to declare peace within yourself; this will stop your ego from continuously seeking war.

CHAPTER 9

The Roles We Adopt

The human oblivious to his Being (Pure Love) falls into a vacuum.
He adopts borrowed roles, with the sole and desperate intention
of avoiding feeling isolated and lonely.

As we go through life, we use false personalities created from fear and adopt a series of behaviors and attitudes in order to be accepted and recognized; in other words, we adopt roles. Starting in early childhood, these roles allow us to act in ways that Mom and Dad, at least unconsciously, expect and ensure their conditional recognition and affection.

Of all the roles we play, the tyrant, the victim, and the hyper-rational encompass, if not all, at least a majority of the destructive behaviors that we manifest in our daily life. Having said that, according to the personality we have constructed, we tend to favor some roles over others, even if sooner or later in our lives, each of us will employ all three.

The Role of the Tyrant

The role of the tyrant involves seeking out a symbolic victim to mistreat. This is a role that the people with whom I work, whether as participants in my courses or in my conferences, have most difficulty identifying themselves with. If asked, none of us would say that we mistreat people.

Are we not people ourselves?

Aren't we all, on many occasions, veritable tyrants with ourselves?

When you force yourself to work at a job that you don't like, doesn't please you, and doesn't enrich you in any way whatsoever; when you sleep fewer hours than you actually need to feel vital and in a good mood; when you criticize and don't accept yourself as you are; or when you eat food that little by little deprives you of your health—aren't you, in all these situations, tyrannizing your body and mistreating your person? Our nature as dual human beings causes us all, invariably, to act like tyrants to a greater or lesser degree, starting with how we act toward ourselves.

Consider for a moment a very common form of behavior: criticizing others.

What do you think leads a person to criticize other people, if not ignorance of his own Power (Heart)?

This lack of self-love leads to both internal and external forms of insecurity and immaturity that need the act of criticizing others in order for the person to feel better. This behavior always seeks to place the criticized party at a lower level than oneself.

It is one of the forms that people estranged from the Reality of their own Loving Being use to feel better about themselves. If the other person is "bad," then at least I won't feel as "bad" or as lonely in my darkness.

People criticize others to feel that someone else is worse off than they are, as a way of not feeling "bad" themselves!

Criticism, mistreatment, contempt, and tyranny only punish those who manifest them, as any injustice committed against others in the end only fuels our own darkness.

REMEMBER: Negative thoughts connect you to dark currents, and your behavior creates experiences of the same energy level; in other words, the person who criticizes others is attracting criticism, judgment, or mistreatment to themselves in some way through their behavior.

We all know, at least inwardly, that something we're doing is not right. At times, the pain is so intense and the sensations so unbearable that to avoid them and face what is not working in us, we spend our time seeking out defects in others, instead. However, it is the perfect time to heal your ego and allow yourself to enjoy life.

The person who tyrannizes others is a person who invariably was tyrannized in some way and could not, did not want to, or did not know how to resolve the issue with his aggressor. There are two reasons that lead the tyrant to act the way he does. The first is an attempt to garner recognition from the person who mistreats him—a need for approval. The second is a way to make someone else pay for his accumulated and unexpressed anger—an act of revenge. If he does not succeed in taking revenge on the person who tyrannized him, who at the time made him feel impotent, he proceeds to take it out on others. Understanding the reason behind this mechanism does not justify the aggressor.

REMEMBER: Each and every one of us has the power to forgive. Forgiveness is characteristic of the Heart itself, and no human can exist without having one beating in their chests.

Forgiveness is an act of the Heart, and your liberation is the immediate consequence.

The Role of the Victim

The victim seeks to elicit pity, the sole intention of which is to manipulate others. This person prefers to complain and accuse others (cowardice) rather than take responsibility (honesty and courage) to find a way out of the situation she finds herself in. The victim always looks for a perpetrator to complain about.

Let me make clear that here we are not talking about real victims of abuse, but about those who look to others to elicit pity and thereby reap benefits. This is the type of person I see least in my sessions, and when I do, their only purpose is to complain and make me see how much they are suffering and how bad other people are (usually their parents) and how good they are.

The majority of people who play the role of the victim feel annoyed or angry every time someone in their orbit tries to show them a solution to their problems. The person who plays this role does not really wish to find a way out of her "cursed" predicament, much less to feel happy. What she does look for is someone who will confirm how much she is suffering and how hard life has been on her.

Surely you have heard the following type of remarks at some point in your life: "Look at the parents I ended up with," "I'm just unlucky," "Life has been hard for me," "You have it easy," "It's easy for you to say," "I'm cursed," "God has forsaken me," "How am I supposed to be happy when my son or my husband... this or that?" "How am I supposed to be happy when as a kid... this or that happened to me?" and so on.

In more than twenty-five years of experience working with people the world over, I have met some who have suffered tremendous abuse in their childhood. The ways they talk about their difficult experiences after many years can be very different, depending on the types of people they are and the relationships they maintain with the luminous part of their Being.

I remember an elderly man from a small town in Spain who came to see me following the death of his wife. During our sessions, he told me that during the Spanish Civil War, the military police had taken away his father to be shot and, at eight years of age, it was his responsibility to look for food for his mother and his five younger siblings, who were dying of hunger. Every day, he would wait until nightfall to go out into the fields, where he would look for roots, herbs, or anything that might serve to sustain his starving mother and siblings. One night, returning from his arduous task, he took his youngest sister, only two years old, in his arms. With a withered look, she asked him for bread as she closed her eyes for the last time.

Desperate and tormented by the death of his sister, he went out hunting for food very early the next morning. Two military policemen on horseback saw him foraging for herbs on a large farm, and seeing what he was up to decided to teach him a lesson. He was only eight years old, but that didn't stop them from tying each of his arms to one of the horses and dragging him along the road for twenty minutes. Once they arrived at the police station, they proceeded to give him a beating and threw him in jail for stealing. They then forced his mother to pay for his release.

To this day, I get emotional when I remember the incredible simplicity of this man, his kindness, his lack of need for revenge, and the lack of resentment as he recounted his painful experience. However, he cried when recalling his little sister, whom he wasn't able to save from starvation.

At no time during the session did he use an accusing tone of voice or show any need for revenge, nor did he complain about what he had suffered or about the injustice and pain of what he had lived through.

Mandy, on the other hand, was a middle-class woman who talked as often as she could about her wretched childhood. To this day, she would cry because of the day her father had taken her for a walk in his cart. She had fallen asleep, and in the meantime her father had gone home, having forgotten about her outside. Upon waking, she realized what had happened and, not daring to get down from the cart, started screaming for help, but her father, working inside the house, could not hear her. Thus Mandy resigned herself to crying about her miserable luck, feeling like a poor and mistreated child. After half an hour, her father realized she was missing and went out to get her. However, he was irritated by her lack of courage and her playing the role of the victim and refused to offer any words of sympathy.

Still, at seventy years of age, Mandy continued to resent him for this, complaining about the cruelty and abandonment she had suffered at the hands of that man. It was as if time and time again, she was wallowing in a pain that allowed her to feel like the victim and continue to accuse somebody. She needed somebody to be responsible for her own emptiness.

Everyone on the planet knows suffering. We always have the Power to choose whether we remain in pain by re-creating it over and over again as perfect victims or retake the reins of our Existence and accept the invitation to grow; to become genuine Children of Life and respectful children and internally grown adults when facing our biological parents. We become examples of Love for others. The Essence in you seeks for you to expand it, to manifest it, just as your darkness seeks to be illuminated.

The person who acts from the energy of the victim is connecting herself to vibrating currents that will re-create the suffering time and time again.

In psychology, the capacity to deal flexibly with extreme situations and overcome them is called resilience. Resilience is nothing more than the immediate decision to instantly refocus on our Hearts, on the good that Life has to offer.

How important it is to teach kids from childhood not to indulge in self-pity every time they are faced with an obstacle, be it a fall, a loss, or any other kind of frustration. It's one thing to cry and release that momentary or permanent pain or feeling of injustice; it is quite another, much more sad and painful, to prolong that feeling.

It is as important for little ones to learn how to release pain, to see in the example of the adults around them that forgiving themselves and forgiving others, if needed, is natural and good, as it is that they immediately recapture their youthful well-being. Children thus educated (loved and respected), when faced with adversities throughout their human lives, influenced by their egos, will doubtlessly choose to get up and resume their paths in the Light, from their unalterable Hearts and vitality. Such children will experience true Happiness and Well-being throughout their earthly lives.

The Role of the Hyper-Rational

The person who plays the hyper-rational role favors thinking over feeling to such an extent that he anesthetizes his emotions. The hyper-rational individual is the one who believes that he is feeling.

I'm sure you've come across these types of remarks: "I believe that I love her," "I think that we should get married," "Well, of course, I love them; they are my parents/kids after all," and so forth.

Look closely at this last comment. How many people maintain that they love their parents only because they are their parents; that is, because society says it is their duty, and they think they must? What does the belief about a duty have to do with a natural feeling like love?

There are people who, when talking about their partners, do so using countless descriptions of behavior and physical attributes, but not using any terms that refer to their emotions or their partners' emotions.

For example: "Mario is a fantastic guy. He's a lawyer. He's very intelligent. He's cute, He's attentive. He's friendly. Apart from that he's got lots of money, he's a great father, he's what I wanted for my children, he takes me out to the finest restaurants, he has exquisite taste in clothes and is very classy." This is a typical description that a hyper-rational woman would give.

Compare this to the description given by a man in tune with his emotions: "Maria is wonderful. I love her like no one else. I feel in love. Her smile makes me melt. When I look at her I feel like one of the happiest men in the world."

Joy was thirty years old when she came to me, determined to resolve her ever-difficult relationship with her father. According to her, he was cold and had never shown affection. Nevertheless, deep down she was sure her father loved her. But for some reason, she had got it in her head that she was the one responsible for this man's behavior toward her.

She felt that she had been insolent or smart-mouthed as a child, and that maybe it had been her who hadn't given him the opportunity to be loving toward her; therefore, she felt guilty and justifiably punished.

After working with me for one session, and more awake to her own Heart and more loving and in tune with herself, she didn't waste a second and went to visit her father. She firmly told him how much she was hurt by the coldness of their relationship and how much she would like the situation to change. Getting no reaction from him, she decided to open her heart by offering him the tender and affectionate hug she always felt she was missing from him. To her surprise, he didn't even bat an eyelid. He simply stood there, immobile, without reacting to his daughter's embrace. She accepted it.

Months later, this man came to see me after having been diagnosed with cancer. Alan, as he was called, still didn't know how to deal with the pain caused by his biological father leaving his mother when he was just six years old, and his father's utter indifference when leaving him.

Joy didn't know about his drama until that very moment. The young woman was finally able to see that the coldness shown by her father had been his way of protecting himself. On the other hand, Alan was able to get rid of the belief of having done something "bad" that had triggered his father's departure. During the sessions, he began realizing that in order to avoid feeling abandoned or betrayed by anyone else, he had simply stopped feeling and stopped loving. He healed his relationship with himself and then dared to share his heart with his daughter and with others.

The Danger of Not Feeling

People who hide themselves behind the role of the hyper-rational end up not feeling. They spend their lives not enjoying well-being; some of them just survive (not live) without any kind of emotion. They do what they have to do or what they think they have to do without taking any feelings or emotions into account.

Taken to an extreme, this role can be highly dangerous.

Many teenage murders, and also many of those committed by adolescents themselves in schools and colleges, are a consequence of not feeling.

These young people have learned and taken the lack of feeling to such an extreme that they are no longer able to distinguish between Light and darkness and end up getting lost themselves.

Take a look at the education that children are currently getting in their free time: television, violence, superficiality, cell phones, and tablets. Consequences? Evasion, absence, vacuum, and addiction.

School-age children spend long hours sitting in a classroom giving exclusive importance to their minds. It isn't only the fact of sitting in the same posture for long periods of time that is damaging to their growing nervous systems and their bodies, but the exclusive focus on their minds to the neglect of their emotions. This invariably leads to a state of suffering that they learn to normalize.

In conventional schooling, we already learn to suffer. Mistreatment becomes the norm; something that is "okay and must be done."

And what do these children do when they get home after a long day in school? What do they do on weekends, on days off, on holidays, when traveling in cars or sitting in restaurants waiting for their meals to be served?

With few exceptions they get hooked on their cell phones, their TVs, their computers, or their video games. Apart from the fact that these activities cause them to evade their emotional and real worlds, the programs on TV and the content of video games encourage children to gradually set aside action in favor of boredom and passivity; to become desensitized, to simply stop feeling. They discourage them from becoming involved and taking responsibility for themselves.

In order to feel, you need first to observe others and to observe yourself, but you can't observe or share with others if you're not present.

A great friend of mine who works as a screenwriter in Hollywood often tells me how difficult it is for her to sell scripts that don't include big explosions, special effects, or scenes that show destruction or make the viewer jump.

The purpose of cinema has always been to provoke emotions. People watch movies to treat themselves to a range of emotions that they would not normally experience in everyday life. In the safety of the movie theater, they can feel without being seen. Currently, the majority of people going to the movie theater belong to the younger generation. Hollywood, no stranger to this tendency, produces violent movies whose emotional intensity is capable of affecting them. The movie industry is aware of the fact that the young audiences, accustomed as they are to not feeling, require more and more extreme impetus in order to react.

Years ago, the personalities of Snow White's seven dwarfs and the tenderness they conveyed were enough to sell a movie and touch a large audience. Today, it is the truly wicked witch who takes center stage. We need aliens, killers, zombies, vampires, explosions, deaths, beatings, gunshots, and myriad special effects to persuade the youth just to go to the movies. Extreme desensitization?

A student of mine who works in a large film distribution company in Los Angeles has the task, among other things, of screening every movie before it hits the big screens. In one session, she told me that she and her whole team of young talents reacted in the most surprising ways—usually with laughter—when watching scenes of terror, horror, or extreme suffering.

Lack of emotion is an evil that threatens this planet, especially in such an intelligent and advanced world, where "knowing" takes up all the space by rejecting feeling, observing, and the inborn teachings of the Heart.

In our children's education, there is no room for observation, free will, or emotion—no room for communicating with the Being. But promoting the follower inside rather than encouraging actions born of free will (personal responsibility) leads to the poor outcomes we later complain about. We discuss these personal or social consequences with our colleagues or friends, while our children right beside us, with their headphones on, can't even hear us. The ubiquitous headphones serve as protection for them against their environment—an environment they can't trust, as so many of the adults they come into contact with complain about something they themselves encourage.

Get to Know Yourself Again and Free Yourself

What is it that incites us to adopt these invariably damaging roles? We invariably do it to imitate Mom and Dad or to play the role they would expect of us. One way or another, it remains an unconscious form of seeking approval. Oblivious to their essence, people choose to adopt such roles as a way of not feeling or believing that they are alone.

The Most Human Behaviors

We humans have tended to repeat a series of behaviors in the course of our history. The following is not an exhaustive list, but simply a guide to help identify the types of behavior you tend to use in your daily life.

ACCUSING: Human beings tend to accuse others and hold them responsible for anything that happens to them. When we have a problem, our immediate tendency is to find someone to blame, even when we are well aware that we are the ones who have made the mistake.

I'll give you an example of a type of behavior that, although it may sound comical, was not so funny for the person who suffered from it.

A few years ago I met Norma, an artist who, after a time, became a good friend of mine. Norma had a hard time owning up to her own mistakes to such an extent that, when she saw that she wasn't right and could find no one to blame, she would say, "Well, if I did this to you, it's because you attracted it." Of course, Norma was constantly attracting others into accusing her, and before long she had no more friends. Her situation didn't change until she understood the consequences of her continuous accusations, forgave herself, and began assuming responsibility for her actions. Yes, making changes is possible!

If you catch yourself accusing others, you could take a few minutes once you get home to be with and observe yourself in order to discover the reasons behind this need in you. Focus your attention on the soles of your feet and ask yourself: "How do I feel bad about myself? What is it that's bothering me about the behavior of this person to the point that I would accuse them? How does it make me feel? What does it remind me of?"

FAILING TO ACKNOWLEDGE: This behavior stems from the previous one (accusing). Every time we accuse another person, we're actually hiding ourselves, failing to acknowledge our responsibility for what has happened because we don't want to realize that we are not perfect as a person. If the other person is wrong, then I'm the one who is right.

In reality, realizing this requires an attitude of humility that immediately offers us an opportunity to make an always liberating change.

Imagine a person who has had a minor car accident and hit the car in front of him. Usually, his reaction will sound like one of the following: "It had rained, and the road was wet," "There was a car coming the other way and blinded me with his bright lights," "The guy slammed on his brakes," "My brakes didn't work," "My car is a piece of junk," "Somebody distracted me," "He shouldn't have stopped right there," "People don't know how to drive these days," "I need to change my contact lenses," "The sleeping pills my doctor gave me are affecting my reflexes." Or, we sometimes go so far as to accuse a part of our own body, "My leg didn't react properly." All of this just to feel that we weren't the ones responsible, that we are not the guilty ones.

Instead, a response dictated by the Heart, free from emotional needs, would sound something like this, "Yes, it's true. I wasn't paying attention and didn't brake in time."

The need for approval and security are at the root of such damaging behavior for those who manifest it. Insecure as we are, we fear that if others discover that we are not perfect, we will lose their affection. Inwardly, every person feels that something is not right in them, but they simply can't stand the thought that others might see it, too.

How much relief we would all feel if we only realized that we are not alone in this fear, that we are not the only ones who feel "bad" or "flawed."

Each time you realize that you don't acknowledge something you've done or something for which you are to some extent responsible, stop immediately, forgive yourself, and recognize your error. It's surprising how many times we believe that somebody is going to reject us if we acknowledge that we have made a mistake, when actually it's the other way around: the more we acknowledge, the more people will appreciate us. People appreciate honesty and humility in others. Why do you think this is?

Imagine that your partner forgets your birthday, and in an attempt to set things right he invents a string of outlandish excuses. Given that he is your partner, you love him and know him well enough to know that what he's telling you is not true, and this hurts you more than the simple fact that he forgot. But what if, instead of not acknowledging his mistake, he simply said, "It's true. I'm so sorry, honey. I just forgot. But what I never forget is the love that I feel for you. Let me make it up to you and take you out to dinner at the romantic place where we first met." Now, wouldn't the result be utterly different?

COMPLAINING: Complaining is a very common practice in all humans. We complain about everything: the weather, politics, our parents, the system, contamination, the poor distribution of wealth, natural disasters, the price of things, God, and so on.

It never ceases to surprise me how many people say "What awful weather!" when it rains, and "What stifling heat!" when the sun is out. When it's dry, they complain about the dryness; when it's raining, they instantly complain about the annoying rain.

Complaining is a way of avoiding dealing with our problems and consequent unhappiness, instead of assuming responsibility and making the decisions that will change the course and rhythm of things. As long as we can complain, we once again feel that there is something outside ourselves that is responsible for our ills. In this way, we remain in the inertia and darkness dictated by our egos. When we complain, we are accusing others, making ourselves out to be good, as if we weren't already good naturally, thus making others responsible for our Happiness, even for our Evolution.

Each time you catch yourself complaining, ask yourself what you can do to change the situation that bothers you so much. Perhaps, at times, it is not a question of changing a situation but changing our emotional response to that situation. Do you know of any child who doesn't like the rain? Who doesn't like jumping in puddles and soaking herself? It may be a question of simply recovering your lost joy in living.

CRITICIZING: Criticizing is so common that, for some families and friends it seems to be the preferred sport, the activity most practiced. Estranged from themselves and their own inner richness, people have little to offer others and little to share. Criticizing others allows them to fill this void left by their own lack of presence.

How bad we must feel about ourselves to have to resort to putting down someone else! The moment we heal our relationship with ourselves and begin to forgive ourselves, the need to criticize others diminishes considerably, to the point of disappearing completely from our lives. Once your ego is soothed, once it feels secure and protected in your presence, it no longer has a need to criticize, nor to compete with or feel superior to others.

MANIPULATING: This is the behavior most often used by those who adopt the role of the victim: manipulating others into doing or saying what suits the victim best. Some manipulate by eliciting pity; others do it with great subtlety and intelligence. If you use this kind of behavior, you will have to pay great attention in order to identify it. A spoiled ego becomes a very manipulative ego. By manipulating, we are assuming that we cannot obtain what we want by means more suited to our Evolution. The moment we decide to take the reins of our lives using our Hearts, the ego's need to manipulate vanishes. When your ego understands that you are there to provide everything that it wants and needs, it subsides and stops sending you messages demanding that you obtain those things by manipulating others.

SEDUCING: Seducing is a very common variant of the manipulative behavior.

PLEASING: People who try to please others need an approving mirror. They act with the sole purpose of gaining a reflection of approval and affection. It is a variant of manipulation, but with its own set of nuances.

You will probably remember having seen one of those commercials from the 1950s that were designed to extol the virtues of the American housewife. These commercials attempted to make women of that era into the perfect servants. They expected women to become the servant that society expected of them: a perfect housewife who would clean, iron, cook, look after the kids, be immaculately dressed and made up and, if possible, refrain from voicing her opinions; instead, repeating those of her husband, with an everlasting smile.

Ask yourself if you are capable of expressing and defending your opinions, tastes, and values, or if you need the approval of everyone to the point of turning yourself into a different person only for them. If the latter is the case, then, as always, forgive yourself and get ready to recover your Power.

BEING SUBMISSIVE: Being submissive is the most extreme form of the need to please others. It consists in submitting to the will of another person, thus completely neglecting your own needs and desires. It is the total negation of yourself, your personality, your identity, and your Existence.

It is the worst form of abuse that we can subject ourselves and our Being to. To do this is the equivalent of putting duct tape on the voice of our Being and silencing it.

Submission creates an extreme inner rage and frustration, which is at the same time silenced and squelched continuously by the choices of the person submitting. These buried emotions have the power to create painful illnesses and, on occasion, dangerous and uncontrollable bursts of anger. You will have heard about those people who are perceived to be calm and nice, only to end up killing someone.

If you see yourself in this painful type of behavior dictated by your ego, don't waste a second to retake control of your life and free yourself from all the frustration that it will have undoubtedly caused by accumulating these submissive attitudes.

ATTACKING: This is the typical form of behavior displayed by the tyrant and has many different and dark facets: subjugating, ridiculing, making someone feel inferior, showing disdain, hitting, physically or psychologically mistreating, abusing, and so forth. On the other hand, it is one of the most easily identifiable forms of behavior, when used.

People who use these behaviors need to identify them and immediately look for the help they need to channel this violence so they can stop it. It is they who are harmed the most by this violence.

In general, the person who attacks others was previously attacked herself, and has not allowed herself to heal the wounds caused by the attack nor face the protagonist. To free oneself from this dangerous reflex of aggression, one will have to dare to face up to one's own buried pain, to forgive others and oneself, to allow oneself to release the anger, the frustration, and the desire for revenge that have rooted themselves so deeply within.

Make daily use of a technique that I have called "Breathe It Out" to release your repressed anger.

REVENGE: Revenge goes something like this, "You've hurt me, so now I'm going to hurt you." This is a kind of behavior that not only has been shared by almost all cultures throughout history but in many cases has been seen as something fair and equitable: the "an eye for an eye" rule of the Old Testament, the *kataki-uchi*, the vendetta, and so forth.

Revenge is the opposite behavior to forgiveness, and therefore against the Light, the Heart, and your Evolution.

The behavior of revenge, so widely accepted and manifested by man, invades the mentality of many societies. Revenge is the basis for western movies: the protagonist is an innocent person who has been attacked and then proceeds to spend the rest of the movie seeking revenge on his aggressor. The most absurd part of it all is that we, as viewers, are left with the feeling that the protagonist has done the right thing; he has done "what had to be done."

Revenge turns those who need it into aggressors. It is a dark form of behavior that can only bring painful results, even if you don't believe it or think it.

If revenge is hovering around your life, forgive yourself immediately, and keep reading. You'll soon discover the practical advantages that forgiveness can yield over revenge at any time in your life.

PROCRASTINATION: This type of behavior is very common among the young and not so young; it produces anxiety and a lack of peace, worry, discomfort, and dissatisfaction in those who engage in it. Who likes to work with a colleague who never reaches his goals, or with a boss who never keeps his word?

Light, expressed affection, that is to say respect, is authentic; it is action and movement; it is creation in motion. Thus, leaving things that you can do today for a tomorrow that rarely arrives is synonymous with sloth and apathy. In no case is it a work of the Heart; it can only bring you unpleasant consequences.

CHAPTER 10

Messages We Have Chosen to Believe

Human beings need to believe in someone and
something outside themselves, as if they themselves were nobody
or didn't have anything to value about themselves.

Having forgotten who he is and what he carries inside—his beautiful and powerful Heart—man feels fear. He seems to be sitting with his back turned to the Love that created him with the sole purpose of enjoying Happiness; the very same Love his Heart treasures. He seems to be sitting with his back turned to the Light that lies in him by birthright as the eternal Son of the Creator Father-Mother he is. This omission makes him lose his lucidity, makes him feel isolated in this small and lost (or maybe not so lost) planet in the immensity of this dark universe.

For centuries, in order to avoid this fear—also caused by a more or less conscious sensation of having been abandoned by God—he has created a series of beliefs imposed by rigid norms, conventions, and references that help him not to feel so alone or so guilty, in order to just survive. "What have we done to God for Him to send us so far away from Himself?" is a question I've heard many times over my years working with people.

But if we want, we can also think something like the following: "God loves me so much that He created me to enjoy myself wherever I choose to go, wherever I choose to experience my existence, without ever abandoning me or imposing any path."

Having forgotten Who we are, and therefore forgotten our Essence, we have stopped listening to the voice of our Being, which in its core of Light is pure Love and Knowledge. Estranged from our Creator Father-Mother, from our own Knowledge, we feel defenseless before that which is the incomprehensible and inexplicable immensity of Life. Led by our egos, our minds show us that we are alone and lost; it is at this point that we begin to adopt social truths as our own and live our lives accordingly, like simple humans devoid of Being.

Some of the social messages that we all accept to a greater or lesser extent and that have greatly influenced the way human beings see their lives are:

- The only life that exists is the one on planet Earth.
- This is the only life that exists and the only one that you will have.
- You must be perfect.
- Your Happiness depends on something outside yourself.
- Everything in this life is a matter of luck.
- Being happy is an act of selfishness and/or a utopia.
- We are only that which we see.
- Illness is something normal.
- We must work long hours to sustain ourselves.
- Society, your parents, and so on are the only ones who know what is good for you.

These mistaken social messages have been seared into the memory of our egos which, to a greater or lesser degree, has led us to believe that they are true, thereby limiting our legitimate Happiness, Peace, and enjoyment of life.

Stay with me until the end of the book and you will see for yourself how to combat each and every one of these messages that have caused so much damage in your earthly existence, at least up till now.

The Messages Proposed to Us by the Ego (Voice of Darkness)

Just as on a social level we are given messages that influence our lives, our ego, too, proposes a series of messages, ideas, or thoughts that have the power to negatively affect our daily experiences.

The messages recorded by our egos speak to us about ourselves, others and life in general.

REGARDING OURSELVES: "You're stupid," "You're clumsy," "Get out of the way," "You'll never amount to anything," "Stop dreaming," "This is not for you," "You can't have this," "If only you were like…" "You're unbearable," "You're just like your loser father," "You're as… as your mother," "Happiness is a utopia; only the rich can achieve it," and so on.

REGARDING OTHERS: "Don't trust strangers," "All men are like boys," "Rich people are all swindlers," "The meek shall inherit the earth," and so on.

REGARDING LIFE IN GENERAL: "Money doesn't grow on trees," "Life is hard," "God is unjust," "We are unlucky," "Being ill is normal," "You have to work hard to be somebody," and so on.

You might be asking yourself: Why should the ego propose these dark thoughts that do us such harm and hurt us so much? How does the ego know what it is that can affect each of us most?

From the moment we are born we are continuously bombarded by messages by our caregivers. Given that our caregivers were themselves oblivious to their true Essence and guided by their fearful and upset egos, the majority of these messages were dictated by their egos and therefore are dark, painful, or limiting.

Messages of Protection
That Your Ego Offers You

Our egos, identifying completely with the dark part of our biological parents, will consider those messages as the only true rules of life. The ego, fearful due to its dark nature, will cling to the messages that it has absorbed in the first years of its life in an attempt to feel safe from life's dangers. The ego will experience them as messages of protection and consistently repeat them to you throughout your life until, that is, you decide to soothe and re-educate it by showing that you are able to run your own life and take responsibility when faced with the problems and difficulties of everyday life.

Do you realize that not only have you been hearing these messages spoken by your caregivers, but by yourself, your own ego, time and time again? They have been etched at an energy level, in each and every one of your cells.

Do you now see why there are so many people all over the world who suffer from anxiety, stress, fear, and depression? How can you not! It is precisely like having someone inside us continuously repeating things that hurt us, scare us, belittle us, and provoke insecurity.

And given that this someone is none other than ourselves, it is a part of us, thus we give it total credence.

CHAPTER 11

Do What I Failed to Do

*Allow yourself to triumph in all that you set out to do, from within,
and with the help of, your infinitely luminous Heart.*

The title of this chapter should really be: "Do What I Failed to Do, But Don't Go Too Far."

Humanity is obsessed with perfection. Inside, we feel a great dichotomy between the core of our Being—the Love present within—and our daily thoughts and actions, which are largely guided by our egos, at least up until now. Unfortunately, this knowledge of our imperfection very often leads us to systematically procreate, to have children, so that at least a part of ourselves may go on to attain the perfection we failed to reach.

Do you realize how different things would be if all beings incarnated on this planet were born of unconditional love and not from the need or belief that we are doing our duty?

Throughout history, humanity has almost obsessively sought to make children similar to their biological parents, education being its tool to achieve it. We create clones of ourselves to be able to identify with them, and we demand that they do what we failed to do. This is an unconscious way of atoning for the guilt that we feel and of protecting ourselves from boredom.

The problem is that while we try to make our children resemble us (usurping the title of parents from the Creator Father-Mother), and demand a perfection from them that we have not attained, at an unconscious level we don't want them to outdo us; we don't want them to surpass us so that we don't feel we failed to begin with.

Can you perceive, even a little, the chaos and confusion sown by these two opposing messages facing off within us? "Be perfect, but don't even think about being better than me."

I recall a fifty-year-old man named Patrick who never drove his car (a convertible Jaguar) when he visited his father so he would not see it. I also recall a woman named Nathalie, a young singer who, a few years ago, was trying to make her way in the French music industry.

Nathalie came to see me, and for all her desire to triumph in music, she couldn't get any producer to pay attention to her or her music. In our first session together, she told me that her mother had also been a singer, and although she was not well known in her country, she had achieved some success in Latin America.

Nathalie's mother had encouraged her to be a singer from a young age: She had her take singing and music lessons and had taught her to act, dance, groom her image, and everything else that was necessary for the future of a successful singer. However, every time Nathalie would speak with her mother about her aspirations and hopes of success, she somehow felt that while her mother was happy for her, she was also saddened by it.

In the very first session, Nathalie was able to see how she had been sabotaging herself in order not to surpass the limited success of her mother. She left the session ready to take on the world, saying she felt free to succeed, as if a great weight had been lifted from her shoulders. And just a short time later she was able to do what she promised she would: Triumph!

REMEMBER: It's not about accusing anybody, or about feeling resentful of the limiting messages that we were given in our childhood. Accusing people doesn't help. It's a behavior rooted in the ego and the role of the victim. It only keeps us away from Love and Happiness. Realizing this is what's important, in order to forgive ourselves, forgive others, and live free.

How many damaged relationships between parents and children are healed by understanding this blind game of our egos?

Allow Yourself to Succeed

Always keep in mind that our Eternal Parents do want you to be happy. They want you to succeed and get the most enjoyment out of your possibilities. This is not only your birthright, but your sole responsibility on this planet.

Remember for a moment this immensely dark universe in which you live. Don't you think it needs all the light that you and each one of us can bring to it? Is turning on the light when you come home at night not a natural gesture? The best way, indeed the only way, to increase your Love

(Light) and that of this universe is to feel happy in each moment. Allow yourself to triumph in everything you try to do from, and with, your infinitely loving Heart.

Your Evolution Asks You to Heal
Your Relationships With Mom and Dad

Healing our relationships with our biological parents necessarily requires the acceptance that you Are and have a Heart, and that your nature as a human being is twofold. It requires acceptance of the fact that they, as human beings, are not perfect, either, and that we are the ones who have been confused by endowing them with godlike characteristics.

Loving somebody is only possible when you see them for who they really are; that is, with their necessarily ever-present flaws and virtues. Precisely those forms of behavior that most irritate you about Mom and Dad are the ones you are imitating and that you promised yourself you would refrain from using before being incarnated. They irritate you because they remind you that you are the one who is not true to Yourself, that you are not being true to the Promise you made to your Parents and to your Evolution.

Some of the students whom I have had the pleasure of accompanying over the years have told me that after previously working with "masters", gurus, coaches, psychologists, or psychiatrists, they had come to the conclusion that to be happy, they had to sever all ties with their biological parents. I've heard comments like: "It's a toxic relationship, and I have to distance myself from them," "They take away my energy," "They saddle me with their problems," "I don't want to feel burdened with their issues," "They get on my nerves," "They unbalance me," "They've always asked so much of me, and they continue to do so," and so forth.

Of course, there are extreme situations in which physical distancing is justified, such as in cases of abusive, psychologically aggressive or violent parents. But in most cases, this distancing is nothing more than an escape for the ego, a way of avoiding having to face our own unresolved issues.

In this earthly experience, we chose a temporary family who could help us evolve by permitting us to experience emotions. We chose this family over any other because it was them, with their features and character traits, who could help us evolve, based on our daily interactions with them. It is in our relationship with Mom and Dad that we allow ourselves to experience the broader range of possible emotions: dependence, admiration, frustration, anger, guilt, deception, fear, and so on.

We chose this family for specific reasons, and it is something that we cannot ignore.

It Reminds Us of What Not to Do

The daily negative behaviors and roles that our parents adopt and expect us to do the same serve as a constant reminder of what not to do. They are a mirror of ourselves, a mirror in which we see our own weaknesses and darkest behaviors reflected. It is like a luminous signal that lights up at each moment and says: "Careful, careful!"

It Helps Us Practice Forgiveness

Whether your biological parents have been authentic to you or the complete opposite, you will always have something to forgive them for, including having been ignorant of their Essence (Father-Mother), of having usurped Their Identity as Parents, and having led you to forget Yourself and Them, thus closing yourself from your Essence and Identity as Eternal Child.

It Teaches Us to Forgive Ourselves

The moment we decide to see and love (if possible) our parents as they really are, with all their virtues and flaws, and forgive them for any type of damage we perceive they have inflicted on us, we will be better prepared to face and forgive ourselves for all the damage that we have done to ourselves.

It Helps Us to Practice Acceptance
of Our Duality – Ego-Heart

Accepting our parents as they are, with their virtues and flaws, Light and darkness, helps us to accept the dual nature in ourselves, our partners, our children, our friends, and all human beings on this planet.

Accepting this dual nature in ourselves and in others frees us from placing impossible demands on others and, in so doing, frees us from the frustration of expecting acknowledgments from others that, in reality, they don't even offer themselves.

It Teaches Us to Love Unconditionally,
Without Expecting Anything in Return

It offers us the opportunity to Love with a capital L; that is to say, to love someone, or at least accept someone, without expecting anything in return, without expecting them to change or to love us back or to behave in ways that we would have wanted them to behave.

Loving is the antidote of needing.

Given that, until now, regardless of our age, our relationship with Mom and Dad has been characterized by an obliviousness of our Creating Parents, and therefore principally from our ego, what do you think has predominated more in your life: Love or need?

As babies, we learn to confuse love for our biological parents with the need for them to care for us and love us.

The ego proposes certain actions or thoughts, and when we accept them, it pushes us to re-create this pattern and continue acting in the same way ("I'm going to love them so that they love me back, because I must, or because it makes me feel safer or good").

Dare to love them, or at least respect them, with nothing in return, nothing more than your own satisfaction in feeling Love or respect.

In certain extreme cases, some biological parents may choose darkness on a daily basis, behaving in wounding, abusive, and aggressive ways. Of course, you are well within your rights not to feel Love for these beings. There's nothing wrong with that. The mind does not decide who we love; it is felt from and within the Heart. If you do not feel Love toward those who manufactured your vehicle, just make sure you don't feel anything bad toward them, either. Make certain that thinking of them does not cause any painful or vengeful emotions in you, such as resentment, sadness, frustration, powerlessness, guilt, and so forth; only compassion.

It Helps Us to Increase Our Light, Grow as Human Beings, and Feel Joy as People

Have you noticed how your ego is always especially active and talkative when it comes to your relationship with your family? Every interaction with Mom and Dad—whether in person, in thoughts, in writing or on the phone—offers a new opportunity to choose whether we position ourselves from our ego or from our Heart, especially when our egos have been pre-programmed to be interested substantially in matters regarding our parents.

As a child you thought that your well-being and personal validation depended entirely on your mom and dad. Your ego took clear note of your belief about needing your biological parents, in order to keep reproducing these messages day after day.

If your situation allows, it is of the utmost importance to heal the relationship with Mom and Dad, to enjoy this reciprocal love and respect that influences your daily life to a great extent.

This does not mean that you should spend all day calling them or keep tabs on them. No. It means that you can share your life with them lovingly and freely, with no strings attached and no dependency, without accusations or feelings of guilt, without expecting anything in return, only offering them your own inborn Happiness transformed into affection and freedom.

If we turn away from the chance to establish a relationship rooted in the Heart and authenticity as opposed to one rooted in submission or hatred while our biological parents are still alive and circumstances allow it, we deprive ourselves of a great opportunity for evolution, to strengthen our Light through our human experience.

Your biological parents don't have to be alive for you to be able to heal your relationship with them. Even if they have continued on their path—what you would refer to as dying—you can still learn to see them just as they were, with the flaws native to the human race.

You can understand that they too were children of ignorance and that each and every action and attitude of theirs toward you was a product of their obliviousness, their experiences, and their own emotional needs and traumas. It is not a question of justifying any type of behavior, but of accepting your parents' duality in order to heal the relationship, liberate yourself, and continue on your path, free of attachment, guilt, and resentment.

See Mom and Dad just as they are or were, without expecting anything from them, then look into your Heart and accept your true feelings toward them.

REMEMBER: Every human being who remains in oblivion of Who he truly is behaves as an Ignorant Being. The ignorance that I'm talking about here cannot be solved by any university created by man.

CHAPTER 12

Forgive Them

*To forgive does not justify the aggressor; it simply liberates you from the
consequences of that pain, giving you the chance
to start a new, healthy, full and fulfilling life, free from
reexperiencing the same suffering.*

Ruth had decided to have sessions with me after having heard me
speak at one of my conferences on health and Happiness. Her personal
situation had pushed her to the limits of desperation. As a child, Ruth
had suffered abuse from an alcoholic father and a silent, submissive
mother who had not known how to protect her.

Ruth had gotten pregnant at eighteen by a man who abandoned
her shortly after the birth of her son. Alone and penniless, she soon
married an older man who turned out to be not only an alcoholic but
also a compulsive gambler. When Ruth's son reached pre-adolescence,
his stepfather began taking his anger out on him in the form of beatings and verbal aggressions. Ruth, ready to protect her son, left her
husband. But after her son left home to pursue his university studies,
her ex-husband begged her to return, and she did.

The truth is, Ruth had come to see me after contracting an illness
of the gums, which was causing their gradual disintegration. Her gums
bled and hurt, and some of her teeth were even starting to loosen. She
felt a victim of circumstance and believed there was nothing she could
do or could have done to change the situations she had lived through.
She attributed all her painful experiences in her past to bad luck and
her unfair fate, and above all she blamed her father for the miserable
life she was leading.

I remember the moment she first mentioned her father. Her
gestures, up until that moment sad and rather defenseless, suddenly
shifted into those of strong resentment, her eyes were livid with rage
and her jaw bristling with tension. It was visually apparent how her gestures and expressions had been completely transformed. She confessed
to intensely hating this man she called her father. She blamed him not

only for her suffering but for the suffering of her mother, who had had to live by his side.

Ruth soon realized that behind the rancor toward her father, in reality, what she still wished was that he had loved her like he *should* have as a father (god). She realized that in her subsequent relationships, she had desperately tried to re-create this love that her father had not given her, or at least had not given her enough of.

However, after some time, she understood that actually her mother *could* have made decisions to get out of her situation and above all done something to protect her daughter from all the beatings her father was meting out to both of them. She was not a woman without resources; she had money and a family that could have helped her, but for her own reasons she had chosen to adopt the role of the victim, a role that she was continuing to play at that very moment as a widow of that abuser.

Ruth cried out of pure rage and also freedom as she discovered that she had been imitating her mother all these years, acting like a defenseless victim, with the sole aim of finding the love that she had unconsciously yearned for all this time. She saw that although her father had been very hard and aggressive with her, he had also been convinced that he was doing "the right thing," as he used to say. And perhaps the most important insight Ruth had come to was that her mother, whom she had always viewed as a martyr, had in reality been manifesting the cowardliness and victimhood generated by her darkness, day after day.

All the shattered pieces of incomprehension fell into place the day Ruth understood that what she had wished for the most (and what had shaped her life until now) was that her father could have loved her and her mother could have protected and taken care of her. She then started an intense effort toward liberating her accumulated hatred and impotence toward her parents, and more importantly, toward herself.

She accepted the invitation to Love, and decided to practice self-forgiveness for the ways she had mistreated herself in an attempt to indulge her biological parents for so many years. A few months later, she had left her husband for good. Her son, happy to see her freed from her painful situation, requested to be transferred to a university closer to where she lived in order to spend more time with her.

Ruth's gums stopped bothering her and her illness abated. She felt so grateful and liberated after her work and recent awakening that she decided to become a coach for women who had, like her, been or were still being mistreated by parents, husbands, or siblings. The years passed and today she lives happily with a person who, as she says, "is not a guy but a man."

Every part of the human body corresponds symbolically to a particular emotion. Illnesses of the gums, as Ruth's case demonstrates, are directly connected to long accumulated rage and resentment and an inability to take the reins of one's own life, thereby abandoning them to others.

One of the things that contributed most to Ruth's liberation was the insight that forgiving her biological parents did not mean that what they had done was right. No, it only showed that she loved herself more than that, and that she did not want to continue perpetuating in the present those painful moments of her past and continue denying herself her present. As a child, her father had abused her and her mother had abandoned her, but as an adult, it had been she who unconsciously perpetuated the abuse inflicted by the models of her biological parents.

Ignorance, a product of our forgetting Who we are and Who our Parents are, leads us, as Ruth's case demonstrates, into perpetuating the very negative forms of behavior that we promised ourselves we would not re-create in this life. You don't have to have lived through situations like Ruth's in order to need to forgive your parents. Locked away in our memories, we all have situations, moments, or attitudes associated with our earthly parents that still hurt us.

The Illusion of the Immaculate

Sometimes I meet people who are not able to identify any aspect for which they should forgive their parents. Not having gotten through the phase of differentiation that adolescence entails, they are still convinced, as a young child would be, that their biological parents exclusively used their Hearts at every moment of their lives, that they are perfect, or nearly perfect, people.

In reality, we are all Light, and we are responsible for transforming the dark side—the one that we have known when we "let go of" the House of God Father-Mother—Alchemy! We all have the same mission living our journey through so-called "eternity" from our awakening Hearts incarnated on this planet, or wherever else in this universe. If you are one of those who thinks that their parents use or used only their Heart, tell me: Did they always treat themselves well? Were they consistently in good health and professionally successful? Were they happy—not just content or satisfied—with their significant other every single day of their lives? Did they enjoy the company of exceptionally kind and loving friends? Did they always know who they were and who their true Parents were, and did they teach you this? Did they educate you from this Clarity? Were they always happy and at peace?

Everyone born on this planet is a human being and, as such, is twofold and imperfect as a person. To those who recognize this from a place of humility and acceptance, it is just a natural process, completely worthy of love and respect.

Dare to Forgive

Forgive your parents for having taught you or encouraged the negative behaviors and attitudes that you have been using to this day. Forgive them for their Ignorance, for having given voice to their ego instead of their Heart, as all of us do. Forgive them for having demanded, in their Ignorance, behaviors, ways of thinking, and roles that were not the ones that would have allowed you to Grow according to the laws and will of Our Creating Parents.

Forgiving Doesn't Justify the Aggressor

A surprisingly large number of biological parents have acted in extremely aggressive, abusive, or degrading ways. Adults subjected to this type of aggression in childhood tend to be unusually resistant to forgiving their parents, feeling that such forgiveness undermines the seriousness of the transgression.

One man, who along with his four younger siblings had been whipped every Sunday by his father, told me once, "Anne, we need a healthy dose of self-love and lucidity to forgive those who have consciously abused us."

Who can doubt the indescribable pain that he and his younger siblings suffered every Sunday for many years as a result of this father's doctrine? We ask ourselves: How can a father do that? How is such a situation even possible? Who is to blame?

Is it the father, whose Ignorance led him to say to himself each Sunday, "Alright, I'm off to my appointment with the whip and my five children?"

Is it the submissive mother, who didn't protect them?

Is it the neighbors, who, having heard them screaming in pain, didn't call the authorities?

Is it the friends and family members, who knew about this despicable act and didn't do anything?

The truth is that what's done is done; it already belongs in the past, at least in this man's case. After we started working together, he quickly understood that all that was left to him was to fully live in the present moment and decide whether to forgive his father or continue to hate and accuse him—and the god he held responsible for his behavior—for the rest of his earthly life.

His anger against the god of his childhood caused him to suffer convulsions and suppressed screams. Allowing memories of pain and injustice to replay constantly in our minds and bodies only causes feelings of powerlessness, resentment, hatred, and maybe revenge. This man was gradually able to let go of the memories of those horrible moments by using his Heart as guidance, allowing him to fully release the painful resentment he felt. Today, he realizes that God, Father-Mother who lives in each of us is very different from his father's god, the one "responsible" for those painful experiences.

Your Heart holds the Compassion that can soothe and heal your vengeful ego. Don't let your ego make you believe that there is something humiliating in forgiving the person who has humiliated you.

Furthermore, understand that resentment, rancor, and victimhood, when you allow them to take up residence inside you, create both physical and emotional illnesses and malaise. They keep you energetically bound to the person toward whom you have such feelings, and connected to the same dark energy current as the aggressor's, as well as previous generations of aggressors. It keeps your ego in a state of restless despair. It distances you from Happiness. It paralyzes your Evolution.

The personal decision to forgive an aggressor is one that liberates *you*, and allows *you* to continue along your path, free, unburdened by pain and impotent thoughts —nobody can change the past. Forgiveness allows you to take back your reason for existing and begin a new life—one derived from the Love that has Created you in unconditional well-being. That is true Richness!

We are eternal Beings, and it is our nature to be happy. During this earthly experience, you are responsible for maintaining the Promise you made to your Parents to spread that Happiness through your thoughts, decisions, and acts of joy and kindness.

CHAPTER 13

The Inherent Guilt in You

You are your only master; the only one you can turn to for answers.
You are the Alchemist on your path. Don't turn your back on yourself.

Consciously or not, human beings seek, and have always sought, Happiness in all they do.

Take babies, for instance. Don't they seek Happiness, joy, pleasure, and satisfaction in every gesture? The moment something disrupts this daily well-being through hunger, fatigue, or wet diapers, they let you know at the top of their lungs. Babies are the most vibrant example of the search to maintain Happiness at all costs. Under normal circumstances, they don't stop until they get what they want, and we all know how persistent they can be!

The Common Quest for Satisfaction Confused With Happiness

The quest for satisfaction, which we understand as Happiness, is the one motivating force in every human being. Have you ever noticed that at the end of the day, everything you do is motivated solely by the goal of bringing you Happiness? Getting up in the morning is in itself an act motivated by Happiness. What do you think will bring you more Happiness—staying in bed all day or getting up and becoming active?

After getting out of bed, you carry out grooming rituals designed to make you feel good about yourself and your body, to smell good and feel fresh. Next, you'll probably have breakfast, eating the food that best nourishes you in order to enjoy living in a healthy body. You must admit that what you're not thinking is, "Let's see. What could I eat today that I wouldn't enjoy?" And if you've decided to go on a particular diet, you do it with the aim of rewarding yourself with something in the mid to long term, maybe beauty, but definitely health.

After having prepared yourself for the day, you'll head to work and perform the task which, until now at least, is the one that earns you money. And why else would you earn this money if it weren't to satisfy your needs and, where possible, your whims?

Unless you have the economic power that allows you not to have to work, I don't think you're saying to yourself, "Today I'm staying at home and not going to work."

On this planet, feeling—not being—happy requires, as we shall see, income, and if possible, lots of it. We could go on listing all your actions and describing how their principal motivating force is personal satisfaction and the attainment of your Happiness.

You might be asking yourself: "So what happens to all those people who stay at home and do nothing, or those who feel victimized but don't do anything to solve their problems?"

REMEMBER: People who adopt the role of the victim have learned that by suffering and eliciting pity from others they will be rewarded. Granted, it is a poor way of reaping an emotional reward—what they would call "feeling happy," if only for one meager moment.

As strange as it may seem, even in war, the ultimate motivation is the search for satisfaction understood as Happiness. The reasons underlying the waging of war can be diverse, but in general they are driven by either an ideological motive or avaricious conquest.

In the former case, those that engage in war will be convinced that they are doing something to please their political or religious leader as well as their "god" and therefore will expect a reward in this life or the next.

In the latter case, nothing motivates the accumulation of territories and material riches more than the hope that those possessions will provide us with something we feel is missing inside, something that we think could fill the void, the result of us forgetting Who we are and our Reality.

Remember, for instance, the quarrel between the two friends discussed earlier. The ultimate aim of a quarrel is invariably to feel happy by obtaining what someone else has, getting a reward, or avoiding a punishment. As we recall, it began with the fact that one friend had forgotten the other friend's birthday. In this scenario, the friend who forgot the birthday defends her position because she doesn't want to lose her friend's affection, and the friend having the birthday wants to recover the affection that she thinks was lost or neglected by her friend.

To Deserve or to Accept

If the quest for satisfaction, or Happiness, is the motivating force behind our actions, why are we human beings not already enjoying Happiness in all aspects of our lives?

Let me offer an answer by way of two simple questions:

FIRST: Do you want to feel happy? If you're reading this book it is very likely that you *do* wish to feel happy in your daily life, as being happy is something that you already are by nature.

SECOND: Stand in front of the mirror, look at yourself intently and answer honestly, Do you feel that you deserve Happiness? The mind will immediately say yes, but is that how you actually feel?

Oddly enough, the majority of people say they want to be happy but don't feel they deserve to be. They feel like there is something "bad" in them that renders them "undeserving" of Happiness. Hence, they see Happiness as something distant and unattainable. In reality, it is not a question of deserving to be happy but of accepting that by nature, you are already happy, and reflecting that by acting from your Source, which is your Heart.

But what mechanism leads us to punish ourselves in such a way that we do not allow ourselves to feel happy to begin with?

Inherent Guilt

Inherent guilt lies within each Being that tours this dark Universe. The Being that experiences itself through its numerous lives tends to feel guilty, as it arrives saddled with all the memories of its past lives and experiences and the results of all the dark choices it has already experienced.

Remember that our Being is a core of Light surrounded by darkness. From within the darkness of our Being, seeing ourselves alone in the dark immensity of this universe, we feel abandoned by our Parents. In reality, we are angry at Love, and we are angry at Light itself as the highest expression of Love. This anger at the Creator provokes in us a perennial guilt.

The human being fears his Light more than darkness.

Unfulfilled Promises

This guilt, inherent in the Being, is reinforced on a daily basis, due to the Being's implicit knowledge that, as people, we are not doing it right—that we are turning our backs on the Creating Essence in us.

When I work with my students and ask them to look at their reflection in the mirror, every one of them, when facing themselves, invariably feels that there is something they are not doing right. They feel that they are not living up to their promises. Most of them feel this way, even if they can't understand why. Others realize that they are simply asleep. Something inside speaks to them and they feel a craving to wake up.

The Role of Education

As if this accumulation of guilt weren't enough, education serves to reinforce it even further. The messages of our educators, and of society itself, demand that we be "perfect" according to poor, and merely human, criteria. These social criteria are far from the perfection we inherently know from our Being. Inwardly, we all have a clear notion of what perfection is—a reflection of our luminous Heart.

The problem is that the very Light that resides in us has been given a voice in solely human terms, within the rigid rules of our education, and in such a way that we cannot recognize it as an echo of our inner selves: getting the best grades in school; obtaining a degree or diploma, which is the product of our mind and not of knowing yourself; going to great lengths to earn money; marrying at all costs and as early as possible in order to have kids, and so on. In the end, we all come out of this conventional education more or less hampered.

How many hours does a child or young person in school have left to be with herself, free from television, cell phones, computers, or other external distractions?

The messages—both unconscious and conscious—that we must manifest a perfection constructed from within our limited human mind lead us to feel guilty. We realize that we are not doing what we came to do— Love—and so we punish ourselves. We then expect from others the same degree of perfection we have come to expect from ourselves. In this way, a chain of guilt and frustration is created, which can only be broken by our making a conscious choice from our Hearts.

If you attempt to behave according to an external social criterion for good behavior, ultimately, it will lack meaning for you, and you will feel that something is amiss. Everybody has the capacity to realize, at any given time, that he is not doing what he promised himself he would do before he was born: to act from the only base that is worth it—Love.

The moment you center yourself in your infinitely loving Heart and observe what it means to act from within your Loving Knowledge, you will tap into an innate potential that would otherwise remain hidden. You will enjoy feeling free to expand your personality and your Identity, which is the product of the Love that created you and gave you Life. You will enjoy the Joy of knowing and not forgetting Yourself, even while you experience yourself in the universe, so far away from your infinitely Loving Creating God, Father-Mother.

REMEMBER: All the answers lie within you. Your Being is a droplet of the Creating Essence surrounded, to a greater or lesser extent, by darkness. This droplet in you is pure Knowledge. My purpose in writing this book is to accompany you in awakening this luminous and latent Love and Knowledge inside, which is only waiting for you to use it.

The Danger of the External Master

On occasion at my conferences, I come across participants who steadfastly defend established social norms which, according to them, we should all adhere to. Needless to say, in our society it is useful and convenient to have norms that permit us to maintain a natural order. Nevertheless, these norms would have been much more beneficial had they been created from the Knowledge of the Heart rather than from the poor and needy ego-mind.

Every norm created from our Loving Knowledge would resonate inside us, and when we put it into practice, we would feel in complete harmony with our Being and the purpose of our Evolution.

Do you know of an external "master" who is better for you than your own Heart?

People, ignorant of the fact that they are asleep and only following others, become frightened of their own Light. In their unhappiness, they seek out others whom they deem more luminous, wiser, or better prepared to tell them how they should lead their lives.

Feeling guilty and in some way inferior, they relinquish their power to these people, who they think can tell them how to live their lives. In an attempt to rid themselves of the responsibility for their own Happiness and evolution, they act according to what others think is best for them. If this should fail to yield results, they can then say, "Well, *he* told me to do it this way. I'm not the one who made a mistake. It was him."

Doesn't it strike you how absurd this is? Why become a follower? Why look outside for the affection and information we already have within us?

During my workshops and conferences, I constantly remind people that the only valid master is the one who resides within. Nevertheless, I still get dozens of emails daily from people asking me specifically how they should live their lives. They insist on me telling them what to do.

My work consists exclusively in accompanying you in the discovery of your own answers. There is not one universally valid answer for all of us on how to live our lives. The only valid answer for you is your own, the one that resides within you.

Notice how the number of sects and their adherents continues to grow dramatically all over this planet. Insecure and vulnerable people, looking for someone to provide them with answers about how to lead their lives, end up finding people who speak to them of masters who will give them what they don't have and make them feel happy and able to reach paradise.

These leaders exploit the void left by a person's misguided quest for external answers, stepping into the role that rightfully belongs to the Essence itself. People who become followers surrender all their power—the practical and material, as well as the internal and emotional—to the guru who guides them. They become followers of something or someone external, thereby straying from their Path and all the possibilities that already lie within, which allow them to create and enjoy the Light of their own Heart.

All humans have this tendency. In some way, we re-create what we did with our biological parents—we idolize them in order to unburden ourselves of responsibility for our own lives.

REMEMBER: Neither I, nor Anne (my physical body), is a master (perhaps we all are), nor do I seek followers. To share my Knowledge with you is natural. It is born from the acknowledgement that you, as "the other," are just another "I" to whom I can offer my love and presence as I receive yours; this is my highest joy.

Above all else, seeing you enjoy and be loved makes me feel happier than, by nature, I already am.

Stop Punishing Yourself

Whatever your mistakes, whatever you've done,
you have the power to choose, at each instant,
to forgive yourself and resume your path.

Having accompanied me up to this point in the book, you will have already realized the importance of forgiving yourself for all the errors committed in your past.

With the humility of your infinitely loving Heart, look at yourself in the mirror and decide to forgive yourself for anything you feel the need to.

Forgive yourself for having sabotaged your Happiness for all these years, for having betrayed yourself and the promises you made before your birth, for having turned your back on your Knowledge by imitating the behavior of others and heeding their messages.

Forgive yourself for having turned your back on the Love that is Life itself, and on your Parents who, with infinite Love, have also created You.

Review all of your errors up to this moment but remember, do it kindly, without judging yourself. You only made mistakes. You are human, and as a human you have a dark side.

It's natural to make mistakes. It's okay. It's enough if in this very instant you decide to forgive yourself.

REMEMBER: Judgment brings guilt, and guilt always seeks punishment. It's no use punishing yourself and allowing yourself to plunge into guilt. Only realize what is happening, and decide to set a new course.

You too have the irrevocable power (a gift from your Parents) of choosing the direction you wish to take in each moment of your life. Of course, it's important for you to see how mistaken you have been until now, and how much damage you have caused yourself or others.

Nobody can correct the mistake in the dictation if the text hasn't been read and re-read. The purpose of doing so is not to feel punished; rather, it is to learn the power and freedom of finally being able to write well, without fear of making the same mistakes. Choose now the well-being that your Heart offers you over your ego.

It Is Never Too Late
to Resume Your Evolution

Sometimes I meet people who think it is already too late. In general, these are people who, having done something "horrible," recognize their transgression and wish to atone for it. However, not being able to erase what happened, they feel they have been tainted, and try as they might, this stain and stigma continues to hound them. They think there is no way out, that they must necessarily remain in the darkness of self-punishment.

The ego! Do you recognize it?

Tom was just nineteen when he came for his first session. He had just been released from prison. A year prior, on leaving a party with his friends and having consumed drugs, he hit a little ten-year-old girl with his car. Her name was Lily, and she died instantly.

The young man was absolutely devastated, and it was not his idea to begin sessions with me. His mother, desperate to help him, had brought him to me. In general, I don't work with people who have not come of their own accord, but I made an exception as I quickly saw that he wanted to free himself from this pain.

He was convinced that his life had ended the day he accidentally killed that little girl. He thought of her day and night and was obsessed with the pain he had caused her parents. He would wake up screaming, anxious, and bathed in sweat almost every night. In this case, the desperation was twofold, because although he constantly thought of ridding himself of the pain by taking his own life, his religion forbade him from this act, and he feared that he would end up in hell if he committed suicide. He felt trapped, desperate, and saw no way out.

Tom's mother, who waited for him anxiously for the three intensive hours of that session, could not believe the change in attitude and morale that had come over her son afterward. But in most cases, it does not require long months of support to wake up to the fact that you are not alone on this planet, to awaken to your Reality and your innate Happiness of existence.

You can do it. And even though sometimes you feel alone, desperate, or incapable of doing anything good and need help, you are "the savior" of your life, as long as you act from your Heart. In your Heart lives this droplet of the Essence, Father-Mother, that has created you. You are the eternal Child of Love, and It in you Is all Powerful.

> Tom did well in the session, and quickly understood that, although what he had lived through was very hard and that that accident would in some form or other remain with him forever, he had the power and duty to forgive himself. He had the duty to return to the Light of his existence, to the Love of his Parents. He understood that his pain was not going to bring back that little girl, nor return her to her parents.
>
> In an "energy planes" session, he discovered that the girl, Lily, who had been a stranger to him until that moment, did not need to forgive him. The Being of the person who was Lily conveyed to him that she had had her own reasons for departing in that way, and in that very instant, and most importantly, she was fine where she currently was.

Before I go on, let me point out that an energy planes session has nothing to do with being a medium, a clairvoyant, or any of those types of profession which, though I respect, I don't identify myself with. The work that I do simply makes use of the multiplicity of vibrating planes that coexist in this universe, in order to, if necessary, communicate with a specific Being that needs help or can help another human being.

> A few days after an intensive session, Tom called me and said that, having felt the need to ask Lily's parents for forgiveness, he had showed up at their door. The mother, still stricken, shut the door in his face. Tom, initially disheartened and then determined, wrote them a letter to express his condolences, and most importantly, to communicate to them what the Being, that was formerly their daughter, had conveyed to him. After quite some time, they called him to talk. He told me about this encounter from a place of great peace and tender emotion, which I thanked him for.

The immense relief that those grieving parents felt at hearing that their little girl was okay undoubtedly helped them, in time, to forgive Tom from the bottom of their Beings. And so it happened.

No matter what you have done, you have the duty and power to choose, at every moment, to forgive yourself and get back on your path. By punishing and harming yourself, you're not going to alleviate any of the pain of the person you've hurt; you're only going to cause more suffering in this already dark universe.

By not forgiving yourself, you remain connected to the dark current of punishment and horror. If there is something you can do to repair the damage caused, it is to regret your act deeply and forgive yourself from your Heart, ask for forgiveness when possible, thus freeing yourself and expanding your Love.

Errare Humanum Est

At other times, I meet people who claim they cannot forgive themselves because in the moment they harmed others they were aware that what they were doing was bad, that they were being bad. They were conscious of the harm they were inflicting. In these cases, if I ask them if they would do it again in light of their reawakened knowledge, barring very rare exceptions related to obsession and mental illness, they say no.

Whatever you may have done in the past, forgiveness is the only energy that can liberate you. If you did what you did at that moment, it was because you were held captive by your ego, you had become your own victim. In all likelihood, you couldn't see how to free yourself by the roles you were playing, by the emotional needs instilled in you since childhood.

In the words of Seneca: *Errare humanum est, sed in errare perseverare diabolicum*. "To err is human, but to persist in error is diabolical."

In other words: Those with knowledge can no longer feign ignorance. To err is something inherent in the nature of the human being simply because it is twofold. Persisting in error amounts to ceding your power to darkness.

REMEMBER: Stubbornly trying to hurt yourself, wreaking revenge, and not recognizing your errors are actions that do not come from the Light of your Heart. Choose to forgive yourself and enjoy your Happiness!

Part Three

Remember How To
Use Your Power
To Create Your Life

CHAPTER 15

Claim Responsibility

Become the beloved co-creator of your Parents.

There was once a boy who lived happily in a lovely and remote hamlet in the mountains.

One day he woke later than usual and hurried out of the house to be on time for school. Doing so he forgot his coat, and the cold weather of autumn made its presence felt.

The boy ran as fast as he could not to be late for his appointment and suddenly slipped on a rock covered in ice. He fell on his back and hit his head hard. Crying and irritable, he was trying to get up when he saw a group of traveling nomads passing through. They helped him to his feet and dressed the small wound on his head. The boy was cold, upset, and in pain. An old woman from the tribe of nomads looked the little boy straight in the eyes and asked him a question that would change his life forever: Did they take away your Happiness, too? The boy looked at her with eyes wide, taken aback and a little frightened by such a question.

The old woman told him of the generations they had spent looking for who had stolen their Happiness. She explained that he would never be able to feel happy again, and that he should join them in their quest for the thief responsible for the fact that they could no longer be happy. The nomads told him that it was possible the thief of his Happiness wasn't too far away, given that the theft had just happened, and that therefore he should begin his search immediately.

The little boy, convinced that his misery had been caused by a thief who had taken advantage of his fall to steal his Happiness, decided to join the group and embark on a quest.

The days passed, and despite his relentless search, he couldn't find the thief who had stolen his joy. In the following months that he spent with the nomads, he visited towns and cities, crossed rivers and mountains, but still could not find the one responsible for his sudden unhappiness.

The little boy grew up longing for his hamlet, his family, and his friends. He blamed the one who had stolen his Happiness for his inability to enjoy his company. With each passing day, he felt increasingly saddened and farther away from being able to reclaim his lost and beloved Happiness.

One day he met a fair maiden. What he felt with her reminded him of what he had felt before he had lost his Happiness. He believed that she could return his Happiness to him, but although the girl loved him, she could not stand the pressure of not being able to offer him that which he so desperately longed for, and left him.

The years passed, and the boy turned into an older man. When he sensed that his days on this planet were numbered, he resolved to return to the hamlet where he had been so happy, for the last time. It took him several months to get there, but it was worth the effort. As he approached the mountain that had once been his home as a child, the now elderly man was flooded with an immense joy. His memories brought pleasurable sensations and long-forgotten emotions back to him. Suddenly, he realized that he was feeling joyful and closer to Happiness than he had felt in all the years of searching with the nomads.

Exhausted, he tracked down his childhood home and to his surprise found it exactly as it had been the day he left it. Seized with emotion, he went to open the door of his beloved home. His heart quickened. He entered the room in which he had spent so many happy moments. There was nobody there, but the fireplace was alight, and he no longer felt the biting cold that had long settled into his bones and embittered his spirit. He sat for a moment in front of the fireplace, lost in memories, and felt an immense Happiness—a Happiness that flooded his entire being. In that precise instant, it dawned on him that his Happiness had always been with him, had been accompanying him at all times. No one had stolen anything from him!

Realizing this, the first thing he felt was a profound rage toward the nomads who had misled him. He felt an intense rancor toward the old woman who with her intense eyes had made him believe that terrible lie that had led him to waste his entire life. He felt like a fool for not having known that he would never have been able to find Happiness outside, because it had always resided within him. He felt the guilt of having left his home without a word of warning to his family, doubtlessly causing them great misery.

Little by little, breathing in once again the smells of his childhood, he returned to his Heart and understood that, in fact, all the nomads had, like him, been victims of deception by others; they were simply Ignorant. An immense sense of peace welled up in him. The old man closed his eyes, happy, and let himself go, in the knowledge that nobody could ever rob him of his Happiness.

Suddenly, the boy heard the mellifluous voice of his mother calling. "You overslept. You're going to be late for school."

The little boy was startled awake. "Mom!" he cried out euphorically. "It was all a dream! Mom, it's you! Please don't ever forget that Happiness is always inside you."

His mother looked at him tenderly and hugged him, with no idea what he was talking about.

Dream or reality? What do you think?

Our education dictates that our Happiness is at the mercy of others. It teaches us that to be happy we need the external world to provide us with a series of things without which we will never succeed in feeling fulfilled or happy.

Our education claims that to be happy we first need to be loved by others and accepted and approved of by our biological parents and relatives; that to be happy, we need to find a partner who loves us and stays by our side our entire life; that to be happy, we need to have descendants; that our Happiness depends on luck or on what one or other god—interpreted by human minds—orders us to do or decides how we should live.

God, Father-Mother, infinitely Loving, the Creating Essence, or however you choose to call It, loves us unconditionally, and to this end it has endowed us with the Power to construct our own reality. Love, Father-Mother, offers us a series of universal rules or principles so that we may create our own reality from our Knowledge, with the intelligence that remains in our immense Heart.

You, and only you, have the Power to choose what you wish to create for yourself, in your life, under the loving gaze of your Creating Parents.

Even though it may sound innocent or hard to believe, the only reason God created you is so that you may exist in your Love and Happiness, the same Love and Happiness that live within you as a base for all your thoughts and acts. He loves us, and the only thing He expects is for us to expand his Love and build our experiences on top of this base of Love through the length and breadth of what we humans call "eternity."

In a following chapter, I will show you the workings of the principles that the Essence has placed at our disposal, and which for years, lost in oblivion, we have been blind to, squandering the power to create a life of Happiness and success for ourselves.

Only You Can Think in You

The moment we seek Happiness outside of ourselves, we shift responsibility for our Happiness on others: Mom and Dad, other people we know, "luck," "destiny," "God," science, and so on.

Let's return to the metaphor of the taxi for a moment. Imagine that, unaware of the fact that he already has a passenger, the taxi driver combs the streets incessantly, looking for people to pick up in his taxi. But of course, nobody can get into a taxi that is already taken.

The taxi driver, now frustrated, continues his pointless and almost obsessive search for new passengers on the outside. At times, he will even meet people who have no need for a taxi and are annoyed at his insistence; at other times, there will be people who do wish to get in the taxi and feel frustrated at not being able to do so.

Do you now see how the taxi driver needs the precise directions of his own passenger?

No matter how much we seek Happiness outside of ourselves, like this taxi driver, we will never find it there. And no matter how much we try to make others make us happy, those people, just like the passengers sought out by our taxi driver, will neither want nor be able to do so. Nobody but you has the power to create your reality and enjoy and live inside you. Nobody can think with your mind or decide for you from within your "I."

As a driver, you have forgotten that the passenger you are carrying is, in essence, Yourself. You always have the option of turning on the intercom, opening the separating window, and re-establishing contact with yourself.

REMEMBER: You are already happy by your very human nature. Maintaining your Happiness and increasing it is also your choice and sole responsibility on this planet.

The Reasons We Fabricate
in Order Not to Feel Happy

Human beings, utterly oblivious to their own genuine nature, fabricate a series of reasons to rid themselves of the responsibility for their Happiness and for manifesting it in their daily life. The moment we shift the responsibility for something as intimate as our own Happiness to the outside world, we justify our unhappiness with an endless number of more or less important reasons, thereby unconsciously perpetuating and increasing the darkness of our lives. In the course of my life, having been in contact with people from different lands and cultures, I have heard every type of reason for which people believe they cannot be happy. "I can't be happy because":

PAST EVENTS: My father was violent with me as a child. People abused me. My mother didn't love me, and so on.

PHYSICAL TRAITS: I can't have kids. I'm sick. I'm not attractive, and so on.

MATERIAL ASPECTS: I don't have enough money. I don't have the house of my dreams. I don't like my job. I need a better car, and so on.

RELATIONSHIP PROBLEMS: I don't have a partner. My partner doesn't understand me. My kids don't respect me. My boss doesn't value me. People are bad. My husband doesn't love me. My mother-in-law is unbearable. My kids are unruly. I've lost someone close to me, and so on.

DISSATISFACTION WITH MY LIFE: Life is hard. I can't catch a break. God has abandoned me. People are evil and dangerous, and so on.

Feeling happy is an experience that no one, however skilled they are, will be able to take from you. Feeling happy is your personal choice in each given moment. Nobody, no matter how much harm they have caused you in the past, has the power to deprive you of your Happiness. Nothing in you or around you can prevent you from feeling the Happiness that resides within you.

At times, I meet people who have suffered painful losses and come to me already certain that they will never again be able to feel happy. The hardest cases are those of people who, having forgotten who they Truly are, and having fallen into the trap of believing that they are the parents, then lose a "child" or a partner.

I remember a couple of young parents who had just lost their one-year-old child. He fell asleep at night and simply didn't wake up. They had been taking medication for one month and having daily psychotherapy sessions when I first met them.

In my private sessions, I only work with one person at a time, so the couple decided that Barbara, the mother, should be the first one to come. The pain this woman was engulfed in was so intense that her husband didn't even think she would be able to speak coherently, considering that the only thing she constantly repeated, over and over again, was, "I'm his mother, I'm his mother. Give me back my child. Please give him back to me."

After relaxing deeply, she accepted my help in re-establishing communication with her Being, something she did naturally and for the first time in her life.

She finally spoke, saying, "I feel like I'm plugged into an incredibly vibrant immensity." The tears of pain began to merge with tears filled with the joy of recognizing Herself.

After some hours of internal self-awareness, she began to speak. For the first time in her life, she realized that she was much more that the body with which she exclusively identified herself throughout her life. For the first time, she realized that we play many roles on this planet, and that these roles are merely that, roles (mom, wife, and so forth), but that the true Parents of life are none other than God Himself, Father-Mother.

She said, "Now I understand that Reality cannot be understood from a bodily function (mind), but rather from our Heart."

From this new and unexpected Peace, recognized and accepted within her, she could feel the Being of the boy who used to be her little boy. It proved to be a luminous moment of liberation for this incredibly tormented woman.

Without recourse to lengthy explanations, which only serve the mind, she simply said, "Now I understand."

She understood that her little boy was at peace with his departure and wanted to let them know that he was grateful for the time shared with his human parents on this planet. Time went by, and Barbara went on missing her little boy, but when she remembered him, it was now with the peace and joy of knowing that, although she could not understand it with her mind, things were okay. He transmitted to her that one day, in another place and on another plane, they would meet again.

Barbara continued her private sessions and, following intense work lasting several months, she not only rediscovered her smile but she felt even happier and freer than she had felt before the loss of her son. That loss had taught her a great deal, and she had even been liberated from a fear of death that had constantly plagued her. If there is something that saved the young woman, it was not me, but rather her willingness to reclaim her path, to rediscover herself and her own light.

She could have chosen to languish in darkness, suffering, and pain, blaming life and bad luck for her misfortune, but she had the courage to use her Heart, and the results obtained from the Heart are always happy ones.

The moments of pain and nostalgia are now the exception in her life, no longer the rule—just like dark stars in a predominantly luminous universe, as opposed to the once tiny luminous stars in a universe of darkness.

Even in cases of painful loss, when people remember who they are and who the Beings are that they once called their "children" or "husband" or "wife"; when they can finally remember that we are all children of the same Essence; when they discover that this earthly life was really only one more experience for this Being, and in no way its whole Life; that this Being continues its evolutionary journey though the universe free of its material body—then, and only then, are they flooded with an immense sense of Peace and harmony and can at last accept the separation.

We always have the Power to change the direction of our path, no matter how dark or somber it has been until now, or how painful our present life is or our past has been. We all have the Power to strike out on new paths that await in the heart of Life itself. And what is the unfailing result? Your total Well-Being.

The Global Consequences of the External Search for Happiness

Have you ever considered the consequences of this external search for Happiness on a scale larger than that of our own earthly lives?

The majority of family problems stem from the belief that someone is not doing enough to make us feel good, or on the contrary that they're doing something that prevents us from being happy.

Wars are born of the belief, in at least one of the opponents, that others are in possession of that "something" that will make them feel better, more powerful or happy, or that it is necessary to fight them because they are evil and by fighting them they will receive divine benediction.

The contamination and the exploitation of the earth's resources also stems from the belief of some people—ignorant of the Reality—that having material riches will make them happier, that given that this is the only life they will have, it matters little if they destroy the planet or not, as long as they benefit from it. We all act like this to a greater or less extent. We follow these patterns, even though they were made by others, and we act without thinking of the harm our daily acts and behaviors are inflicting on the planet. We behave like those who prefer not to look in order not to see, who prefer to abide blindly by what others have dictated.

Illnesses and epidemics come from the belief that our well-being completely depends on external factors over which we have no control: viruses, bacteria, plagues, and so on.

It is all the more important that we reclaim responsibility for our own Happiness, and stop blaming other people or external factors for our own choices and outcomes.

The decision to be happy is yours and yours alone. Choose it!

CHAPTER 16

Your Mission and Your Purpose

*Nothing has more power to elicit Happiness
than the accomplishment of your mission.*

Just as the blood of your biological parents, Mom and Dad, runs through your veins, so too are you continuously nurtured by the unconditional Love and Knowledge of your Creators: Mother and Father.

If I can awaken you to your Happiness, You and only you have the duty of keeping yourself open and watchful for it. The Purpose of your Being throughout the course of its infinite lives has always been and will always be to love in order to evolve (returning Home to our Parents) throughout your so called "eternal" universal journey. Having decided to incarnate itself in your body, your Being chose to continue pursuing its Purpose through its earthly mission: to share and expand its Love and Knowledge through its presence and Happiness.

For some people, this specific, personal, and unique form of continuing to illuminate their darkness will take the shape of one of the arts, such as music, painting, dance, or writing; for others, it might be serving other people, such as those who, having lived through traumatic experiences, continue choosing the paths toward Love and Happiness; for others, it might entail being an example of joy and humility despite great external wealth; for others, simply making people laugh; and for still others, it might be cultivating the best produce and preparing the healthiest and tastiest meals.

Sharing and expanding our Love and Knowledge through presence and Happiness can take endless forms.

Each and every one of us has a special mission. This mission was the promise we made to our Parents, but few of us remember what it is or that we even made it.

My mission in this life is to awaken people to their own Happiness, while lovingly and attentively nurturing my own.

This is what I had come to do and manifest in this earthly experience. Nevertheless, for many years of my life, "Anne" resisted manifesting that

Happiness (now it is Me, "I", that speaks), resisted putting it into action, at least in the way in which I had promised Our Parents I would.

Sharing with the world my particular but utterly natural way of seeing and perceiving Life and Reality (as a little human girl) was no easy task, and I knew this. On the one hand, I could sense that even though the I in every human being was willing to take the path back toward our Parents, the people in whom they were incarnated were not prepared to listen to what I had come to communicate to them.

On the other hand, and for a long time, Anne was reluctant for me to awaken her fellows to Happiness.

The experiences my person lived through in the first years of her life taught me that, at least as far as the Beings around me were concerned, they could not share that Happiness because they were totally asleep, bogged down in their personal histories.

So, when my body turned nine years of age, I resolved to remain silent. If I stopped talking, I wouldn't be exposing my small body to disappointing trials for being different. Within a religious family, there were certain things that one shouldn't say, among which were: "God doesn't punish." "We're already eternal." "Only God is Mother and Father." "Sins are the invention of people," and so forth.

But when a little girl sees that her biological parents are trapped in forgetting and ignorance, how could one ask her not to try and awaken them, to help them get out of the Ignorance that confounds them about the true origin of human beings?

My silence continued for many years, years in which I tried to make myself heard by sending my body all manner of signals.

The first important warning that I gave Anne occurred when she was twenty-eight years old, when she fractured two vertebrae while doing some exercises on horseback. As Anne awaited her turn in training, she felt my warning and heard me, because she said to a friend, "And what if I were to fall off the horse now?"

But at that instant, she decided to ignore me and got ready to carry out the demanding drill that she had done perfectly so many times. A few seconds into it, she fainted and fell off the horse and onto her back. Later, in the resuscitation unit at the hospital, they tried to prepare her for the possibility that she might never walk again.

A month later, while I (now it's Anne who writes again) was walking out of the hospital on my own two feet, I decided to write a book, a novel, that would allow at least a glimpse of what I had come to share with my fellows. The writing of this novel paved the way for a second and then a third one. However, when I focused more on writing and getting my message across than on getting published, my Being sent me the second vital warning: In addition to having barely 9 diopters of vision in the left eye, I lost the vision in my right eye completely. In short, I could hardly see at all.

I was taken back to the hospital, and they told me that this was the result of a congenital toxoplasmosis, that my eye was severely damaged, and that I might not recover my vision. While they were preparing me for a life of disability, I immediately focused on my Being and heard it say to me, "Don't be afraid. You'll recover your sight soon."

Following this new message, I decided to take another step in the execution of my mission and began offering private sessions in Bordeaux (France). A week later, I could see perfectly. To this day, whenever I have to visit an eye doctor on my travels, they are bewildered and want to run all kinds of tests because they cannot explain how I can see, and moreover without the aid of glasses.

Before proceeding, let me remind you that everything that I can do and have overcome is something that you too are equally capable of.

That which we commonly call "miracles" in general are nothing more than the conscious and deliberate use of the Power of the Heart in you, of your Knowledge, the eternal and inherent treasure in your Heart.

Although I had decided to begin sessions and to convey my message in small gatherings (or as we call them in France, *Petit Comité*), deep down I knew that this wasn't enough—that it was no more than a fraction of what I had come to do.

A few years later, I got another warning: a small heart attack, from which I recovered unscathed, without taking any medication.

Nevertheless, I still wasn't willing to dedicate myself and expand my work as my Being and Life had asked me to, for which I received another signal. One day while preparing my suitcase to travel to the Canary Islands to get together with my siblings, I suddenly saw myself lying in a room with two white beds: a hospital room!

Later, on the plane, I once again saw that image with complete clarity, and once again, I didn't react to this new warning. Two days into my vacation, I tore the ligaments in my right knee. This immobilized me in a room with two white beds for a month. Determined now, I resolved to broaden the scope of my work and offer sessions, seminars, and conferences, not only in France but in neighboring countries as well: Spain, England, and occasionally in Germany.

During this period of time, while living in England, I received an invitation from Spain to run a seminar in Madrid. It was my first seminar in Spanish. I fell completely in love with that country. I must say that I was overjoyed to see that the people there were very open to and welcoming of change.

Following that event, the requests for seminars and private sessions began flooding in, and what I thought would be a weekend in Spain turned into six wonderful years of my life. Still, I was well aware that this relative success was only a minute part of my mission: to awaken Happiness.

My message was Loving, and I was willing to let it be known on a much larger scale. Writing a book and making it known the world over was then the most important step to follow.

And yet my ego kept assailing me with the same doubts and hesitations: "Don't open yourself up to the world," "People are not ready to listen to you," "Every time someone has wanted to bring a message that would truly serve the Eternity and Happiness of Being, all they've achieved is to create a multitude of followers, and you don't like to be followed, do you?", "Don't force yourself," "It's not worth it," and so forth.

This was the moment in which my Being laid down an ultimatum: a brain hemorrhage. One warm summer morning, after having swum underwater for a long while in the pool, I felt an unbearable pain erupt in my head. I instantly knew that the time for a decision had come: to leave this body and continue on My path, or to decide to become Who I was. At that instant, I spoke to my Heart and said, "Here I am. I'm here for You, and I choose to manifest You in the best possible way I can. I agree."

In the ICU bed, I heard the doctors and nurses talking about how my bed would be free to accommodate another patient soon. Due to the brain area affected, and the amount of blood lost, it seemed impossible that I would survive, let alone recover. They even asked my partner to sign the necessary documents determining what to do with my body.

Six years have passed since that brain injury. I recovered from it within a month, without any negative consequences or medication, although it did offer me space for rest and recovery. In that time, I wrote this book and prepared my move to the United States, among other things. I am ready and willing to manifest my Knowledge, making my message available on a scale which I promised myself I would. Happiness opens my path.

REMEMBER: I am only responsible for what I say, not for how people interpret what I say or how they decide to act on it.

Do you remember what your mission is? Do you remember what you came to this planet to manifest? What fuels your passion and gives you joy? What would or does, in fact, get you out of bed in the morning in high spirits?

Eric was a young French policeman who came to see me, ready to change his profession. He said that being a policeman no longer fulfilled him. After a session, he decided to become a firefighter, and in less than a year he had joined the fire department in his city.

Having only had one session with me, he had not fully explored the possibilities that his life had to offer and had not discovered what his real mission was. Two years later, he came back to me to continue his evolutionary work because his new profession did not completely satisfy him, either. Although the money was good, and it allowed him considerable leisure time, he felt something was still missing.

He quickly realized that what he had always wanted to do was act, to be an actor. His humble origins had led him to view these aspirations as a simple dream, a sign of immaturity, something beyond his reach. This time, he didn't hesitate and embarked on regular acting and English classes in addition to his work as a firefighter. With every passing day, he felt happier and more alive.

A few months ago, he took a step that years ago would have been unthinkable: he went to Los Angeles to perfect his language skills and study acting. His surprise was all the greater when he realized that his mission was not only to act and trigger emotions in others but to serve as an example to his biological parents and sister. His humble parents and sister, never having been out of their home town, found their curiosity and desire to enjoy life awakened simply by watching Eric travel to distant places and follow his dream. A week ago, the young man called me to tell me that his parents, having saved up some money, had decided that once retired they would travel and discover the world.

It is true that for Eric, a young and single man without family obligations, making changes in his profession was less complicated than for those saddled with more responsibility. Sometimes, I am faced with heads of families who are burdened with heavy loans and mortgages, feel frustrated in their jobs, and wish to change directions. They are afraid that they will lose the income provided by their present profession, but above all else, they fear encountering the disapproval of their significant others and relatives.

It doesn't matter how long you've ignored your mission, there are always ways of combining it with your current life or finding creative ways to manifest it.

The day I met Claire she was working as a lawyer in a prestigious firm in Paris. At the time, Claire was a single mother and had studied law at the urging of her father who was also a lawyer. Ever since she was a child, she had taken for granted that she would become a lawyer, but she had never seriously considered whether that was what she liked or what would fulfill her.

She came to me because of a depression that she couldn't seem to overcome, despite the medication and therapy she had been on for a few months, and also to address a pain in her upper back.

This woman was passionate about ecology and the protection of the planet and felt that her mission had something to do with the preservation of the environment, without knowing exactly what that might be. During our sessions, I accompanied her on her journey toward discovering what she wished to do, so that she might allow herself that very important change and be able to find the job that was ideal for her, a new job that would allow her to feel happy at last and earn money in the process.

Within a month, a renowned ecological organization contacted her, offering her an interesting position in their legal department. At first, the pay was less than she had been used to, but the hours were much more respectful of her life, more reasonable, allowing her to enjoy more personal time too and time with her kids. Claire wasted no time and used her new-found free time to write a book on ecology, law, and spirituality. The earnings from her book went a long way toward making up the difference in income.

Claire's case demonstrates that we don't always need to make radical changes in our lives; we can apply the changes we make within our current profession.

Stephanie was a young single woman who, although she loved her job and had no intention of leaving it, felt that something was missing from her life. In her company, it was impossible not to laugh—her sense of humor was as natural for her as it was contagious.

No more than two sessions were needed before Stephanie made her decision, and now she combines her daily job with weekend standup performances in a club as a comedian. Nothing affords her more pleasure than making others laugh. The sensation of emptiness that was hounding her has vanished.

It doesn't matter how many years you've spent turning your back on your mission, you can always reclaim it. The present belongs to you, and you have the power to shape the future as you see fit.

Christophe had just become a widower. At eighty-five years of age, he was very apprehensive about death. Seeing the hour of his departure approaching, he felt fear, sadness, frustration, and powerlessness. This man confessed that he had the feeling there was something he still had to do, something that he had not yet done. He told me that he didn't feel ready to die yet.

Only a few sessions sufficed to remind him of Who he was and why he was on this planet, whereupon the paralyzing fear of death he had felt until now was lifted. After a couple of weeks, he felt prepared to continue on his path free from his human body, and at the same time encouraged and filled with the desire to enjoy what time he had left of this life.

Having spent eighty-five years oblivious to his Heart and Happiness did not prevent Christophe from rediscovering the Peace of his Heart. Together we drew up a list of all the things he wanted to do. The first thing he did was learn how to paint, a hobby that he combined with a trip to Patagonia, a cruise through the Norwegian fjords, a photographic safari in Nigeria, and a stay at a spa in Thailand. Before leaving his body, Christophe gave me a lovely painting that he himself had made during a stay in the Swiss Alps. It always brings a smile to my lips when I look at that painting hanging on a wall in my house and read the inscription dedicated to me: "To the person who taught me—yes, yes, don't be mad. I know you simply reminded me and didn't teach me—how to live. My profound and eternal thanks."

If you still don't remember what mission you promised yourself to fulfill in this life, that's okay. Your Being lovingly holds the answers within you. Presently, I will show you how to re-establish communication with your Being. Until then, allow me to speak to you of the principles that govern this Universe.

CHAPTER 17

Universal Principles at Your Service

God, the infinitely Loving Father-Mother in us, invariably endows us with the Power to co-create through our experiences.

We are all born with an internal "instruction manual" that tells us what to do in order to re-create the life we long for. But frequently, we encounter problems because not only do we not realize that this manual is already inside us but we do not know how to read it. It is, in fact, just waiting for you to recognize and use it.

This inner instruction manual contains the principles that govern this universe, what their impact on our lives is, and how to use them to our advantage. Indeed, the Creating Essence has endowed us with the Power to construct and select our experiences and given us the exact and necessary Knowledge to do so. It has placed at our disposal its universal principles, its laws, and rules that allow each of us, without exception, to construct our lives the way we wish to live them.

Remember the Universal Principles

Life has endowed you with all the ingredients necessary for you to manifest Happiness and enjoy living, but what good is it if you can't remember them? Imagine you are seated in front of the world's best chess player, equipped with the best chessboard, the best lighting, the best chess pieces—do you think you could play chess if you didn't know the rules?

Imagine two soccer teams in a championship final. The spectators watch closely from bleachers separated from the field by enormous, soundproof glass partitions. As they walk out onto the field, the players forget everything. Not only have they forgotten what the rules of the game are but they also don't know what game they are playing; in fact, they have no idea what they are even doing there. It is likely that they will spend the next hour and a half sitting on the grass, killing time, or even break out into a fight. Some of them might simply wait for someone to tell them what they should be doing. Eventually, one of the players might even give the ball a kick. But there's an enormous difference between kicking the ball and playing a genuine soccer match and getting the most out of their training and the field itself.

That is precisely what the human being does. He is given an immense playing field, which allows him to create his ideal life in all its aspects, but he has forgotten how to play, forgotten the principles and rules that would allow him to play and achieve what he aspires to. He has even forgotten that the sole reason he finds himself on this field is simply to play with Joy.

The principles that govern the universe are the rules of the game in our lives. To relearn how to construct and enjoy the life that you desire, you will have to recall not only what its principles are but how to go about using them to your advantage.

Below, I offer you a simple list of acceptable or comprehensible principles from the human mind. Although there are other governing principles as well, in this marvelous experience of your Life, the ones I will present to you are the only ones you need at present to transform your existence and begin to enjoy a fulfilling experience. I repeat, this is not an exhaustive scientific treatise examining the principles that govern this universe; it is a reminder that will accompany you on your path through your life on this planet Earth.

THE PRINCIPLE OF EVOLUTION: In this universe, everything has a tendency to evolve. The Being wants to return Home; that is to say, it wants to experience Love through its earthly experiences in order to return to its Parents.

THE PRINCIPLE OF DUALITY: This universe, like everything that exists in it, has a dual nature: Love and Ignorance.

THE PRINCIPLE OF INTERCONNECTION: Everything is made of energy. From your material body to the light from a light bulb, everything is made of atoms of light. All Beings emanate from the same source and are interconnected, united by the droplet of the Essence that inhabits us, creating an infinite network of Loving interconnections that are more or less luminous.

THE PRINCIPLE OF LOVE: Love—that is, Light—is the only fuel that exists in this and all other infinite universes that coexist. Love is what permits us to plug ourselves into one current or another and is what accompanies and allows us to travel, as Beings, from one planet to another, from one galaxy to another, from one universe to another.

THE PRINCIPLE OF CO-CREATION: We are the co-creators of our own worlds and realities. Every event, every situation, every circumstance in our lives has materialized, created by our emotions, sensations, and thoughts, whether we are conscious of it or not.

Quantum physics has established that emotions, sensations, and thoughts have the power to alter the present. With every thought, intention, and desire, we are creating our reality. We are co-creating new worlds. We create what we focus on here on Earth, and to an extent far beyond what we can even begin to imagine. You probably already knew this. But how do you feel about this reality?

You Have the Right and the Duty to Create Your Experience From Within the Love and Light that Lie Within Your Heart

These are the principles that allow you to co-create, construct, and bring about the life you seek. Like the lost and confused soccer players, without these principles, you will not know what to do with what you've been given. You will not know how to benefit from your life or how to create your reality. You will feel defenseless and will believe that things happen to you by chance.

There was once a kingdom in a world far away from ours, in which a prince, heir to the crown and to an immense fortune from the king and queen, had just been born.

The adviser to the king, a wise and powerful man mindful of his awakened Heart, did not know how to awaken the royal couple to the tremendous injustices they were committing against their people. He therefore hatched a bold plan with one sole purpose: to make the new prince a humble man, mindful of his Heart, kind and generous toward his people. To this end, he knew he would have to take him away from his parents and from the education to which they would subject him.

Taking advantage of the darkness offered by a new moon, the adviser took the newborn prince and entrusted him to the care of a humble peasant woman. He gave the woman precise instructions that under no circumstances was she to reveal to the child who he really was. Before leaving he placed a special locket made of tin around the baby's neck. The moment the prince chose to listen to his Heart, the mysterious locket would open, revealing to him the truth about who he was and the size of his fortune.

The royal couple, devastated by the disappearance of their infant, did little but cry about their loss, tortured by the feeling of injustice, although they continued to shirk their responsibilities toward their people.

The years passed, and the prince grew into a humble peasant. He learned to till the land and to complain as many of those around him did. He complained about the bad luck he had had to have been born poor. He complained about how unjust the monarchs were. He complained about the rain, which he blamed for rendering his task even more arduous. He complained about the blazing heat of the sun for the same reasons. He complained about droughts. He complained about the meager harvest... The young prince, ignorant of his origins and his power, always found a reason to be filled with bitterness, frustration, rancor, and resentment. Worse still, he was convinced that there was nothing he could do to change his circumstances.

The adviser, disheartened at seeing that his plan wasn't yielding results and that the young prince was not becoming the future sovereign that he had long hoped he would be, decided to pay him a visit. He himself would try and awaken the beauty of his Heart. On his way there, however, his luxurious and extravagant attire provoked the envy and resentment of some who, out of vengeance, assaulted and killed him.

The prince, connected to the darkest currents of resentment and bitterness, spent his life as the wretched peasant he believed himself to be.

His hair had already begun to gray when his adoptive mother passed away. On her deathbed, he took her hand and looked upon her with tenderness, remembering how much this woman had done for him.

The instant he felt Love in his Heart, the pendant opened. From it fell a small parchment, which unfolded in the air and revealed his true history. Tears streamed down his already wrinkled cheeks as he realized that he had squandered his life by not choosing to exist with his Heart.

Nevertheless, he was also happy, because he knew that his life had not been as wretched as he had believed and, in particular, because now he understood that he would always have the most powerful tool at his disposal to avoid suffering: his Heart.

Human beings generally behave like the prince who was ignorant of his own fortune. He toils through life with considerable sacrifices, ignorant of the fact that he possesses all the riches he could desire and all the tools to bring them to fruition. Confused by his ego, time and time again, he re-creates the experiences that each day estrange him a little more from his true Knowledge, from the possibility of evolving and feeling Happy.

Human beings unknowingly create unpleasant experiences and perpetuate their misery and suffering when they forget they are Children of God Father-Mother, the owners of their existence and creators of their experiences. Like the prince who is oblivious to his origins and birthright and connected principally to his ego and bitterness, their thoughts influence and create their reality.

The Different Realities That Co-Exist

Our limited human senses make reality appear one-dimensional, with defined spatial-temporal boundaries. Reality, however, is very different. Not only do several realities co-exist, as do various worlds on the same planet, but there are an infinite number of co-existing and overlapping universes. As energy Beings, we too co-exist simultaneously on various planes, in various universes. This subject is beyond the scope of this book, though, and what I wish to convey here.

Our five senses allow a limited vision of reality, but even if we just use these five senses, we can still realize that there are different experiences and realities that co-exist on Earth. Even now, on the French Riviera in the south of France, where I am writing this book, there are co-existing realities so different as to appear as different worlds.

For example, the reality of a wealthy retired man, happily married, who peacefully enjoys his lovely house surrounded by trees, dedicating his time to walking, playing golf, going out on his boat, and eating in delicious restaurants with his wife and friends; the reality of a young woman recently arrived from her native land with a husband who abuses her, as a result of his religion, and does not allow her to leave a cramped and run-down rented flat; the reality of a beggar who waits for his earthly life to end;

the reality of a young, or not so young, man who just robbed an old lady to buy the drugs that allow him to blot out his existence from the face of the Earth a bit more every day; the reality of a civil servant who is bored with a job she does simply to earn money, assist her husband, and support her family; the reality of the rich entrepreneur from eastern Europe, traumatized by his experiences in both childhood and adulthood, who spends his days drinking alcohol and smoking cigars in his house; or the reality of the scientist who pollutes the planet as much as he can every day, yet only buys organic products.

If we put ourselves in the shoes of these people, does it not seem that they live in totally disparate worlds? And yet, they all live no more than 500 yards from each other.

And if we apply these examples on a global scale, we see the immense range of realities that co-exist on this same planet. We see the difference between an adolescent from an affluent family in Los Angeles and a person from a hamlet in Congo, or the difference between a successful thirty-year-old woman working in journalism in New York and a woman of the same age living in a conservative African family, or one of the "untouchable" women of India, or one who works in a sweatshop in China.

The differences that co-exist in this world are abysmal. The realities are as varied as the vibrations of energy currents into which you plug yourself in every moment. Some live through relatively peaceful and pleasant experiences, while others literally live in an incessant atmosphere of abuse and extreme suffering.

You Have the Power and the Duty to Choose Which Reality You Wish to Create in Your Life

What makes these people's lives so different from each other? What have some of them done and others not done to have created such divergent life experiences?

The difference lies in the energy currents of differing vibrational levels into which they choose to plug themselves. In other words, it's as if you are walking through movie sets at a large Hollywood studio and you are able to choose one of them to live your life in. What would you choose? *The Notebook* or *The Hunger Games*?

Yes, you can choose which type of movie you wish to live in. And now that you see it more clearly and remember that you have the power to create your life, what type of reality do you wish to inhabit?

Ugliness and beauty, love and fear, joy and sadness, abundance and poverty—they all co-exist, simultaneously, in the same place. They are different realities that share the same spatial-temporal dimension. You simply must decide in which of these realities you wish to live, into which you intend to plug yourself. Indeed, it is as easy as it is powerful.

Allow yourself to be aware of these different realities and myriad multiplicities in daily life, and pay special attention to those which you yourself wish to experience. Deliberately choose your thoughts, learn to soothe your emotions, and always focus on the Light in your Heart. In this way, you plug yourself into Love, well-being, humility, wealth, joy, health, abundance, and other positive energetic currents.

You are on the road to creating a new Reality for yourself with the unconditional support of your Heart. Now it will be easier for you to plug yourself into more luminous currents by way of your thoughts, sensations, and emotions and to make requests of your Life, for it to aid you in creating a new reality and enhancing the vibrational level of your emotions.

CHAPTER 18

Guide Your Thoughts

Darkness is the habit, whereas Light emanates from your Heart,
thanks to a conscious and deliberate choice.

What, in your view, predominates on this planet: suffering or well-being? Look closely at the populations living on each continent and their living conditions and tell me: Are there more people suffering or more people living a life that is naturally pleasurable and happy on this planet?

The universe in which we live is predominantly dark, and so too are the people who inhabit it. Negative energy currents—ignorant thoughts, emotions, and behaviors—predominate.

There's no reason to be alarmed, though.

REMEMBER: Darkness is not bad in itself. It is nothing more than that side of Essence that has not yet been experienced by Love, by a more luminous, incarnated Being—you, I, or any of us on this planet—passing through that darkness and illuminating it.

Given that there are many more dark currents than loving-luminous ones, it is easier to plug yourself into the dark ones than the luminous ones, especially if you are not aware of Who and where you are. In other words, darkness is the normal state here, while Light is the traveler and his conscious and consistent choice of producing Love along his way.

REMEMBER: Each time you plug yourself into a luminous current through your own Light, you are building a happy life, not only here but also in the other planes inhabited by your Being. You are helping to make this cold universe a little happier.

The Importance of Paying Attention
to Your Thoughts

Around 80 percent of the thoughts people have throughout the day escape their conscious minds completely; and these thoughts create their experiences on automatic pilot. Given that darkness is more present than Light in our lives, it is not surprising that this automatic pilot and the thoughts it offers us will also be predominantly dark.

All of your thoughts, whatever they may be, have the power to create your experiences. It doesn't matter if they are unconscious thoughts, thoughts on automatic pilot, thoughts deliberately created through your ego, or loving thoughts created from your Heart—they all contribute to building your reality.

But what happens when people continuously create their reality through dark thoughts on automatic pilot? The consequences are frustrating and demoralizing. They feel betrayed, tricked, and unable to understand how the painful experiences in their lives come about.

The automatic nature of your thoughts will not cause any problem if you remain present to Yourself, knowing that it is You who thinks and decides for yourself. But the moment you abdicate control of your body, senses, and functions, you cede control to your fears and negative thoughts, and they will be automatically and immediately absorbed by darkness, creating considerable constraints on your daily Happiness.

To Change Your Life, Change Your Focus

When creating your new experiences, it is vital that you be as conscious as possible of what you are thinking, and consciously choose what to think, what to think about, and how to think.

The moment you feel any kind of distress, stop and attempt to identify the thought that is circulating through your mind; it is certain to be the cause of your negative sensation or emotion. Once you've identified it, you'll be able to reconstruct your experience by replacing it with a new creative message that you have chosen to use from within your Heart.

Let's take an example. Imagine you get up in the morning and looking out the window, you see that it's raining. Your automatic pilot thought might be: "Yuck. What horrible weather!" and immediately feel sadness or perhaps apathy.

But if you are aware of your negative reaction to the weather, you can stop when that negative thought arises and voluntarily shift your focus. You can say something like, "Hmm, it's raining, and that's exactly what Earth needs," or "Hmm, I love the smell of wet earth," or something similar.

Now imagine that you go to have breakfast and realize that you've forgotten to buy jam. Perhaps you say to yourself, "Again! Always the same. I'm a scatter-brain. I can't do anything right," or "What a pain!"

Here you can consciously choose to stop those thoughts, and instead, think something like: "It's alright. No big deal. It just slipped my mind.

Next time, I'll pay more attention. I'll take advantage of my trip out to visit the new health food store that I've wanted to see for so long and pick out a healthier jam." The current you are now focused on will be of a totally different vibrational level, and so will your experiences.

I remember Timothy, a middle-aged man. He came for sessions with me after deciding to get a divorce and fearing that he might lose contact with his two daughters. His wife had threatened to make his life impossible should he decide to divorce, saying she would convince the judges that he was a bad father and that he should not have contact with his daughters. She came from a family of judges and lawyers and had managed to intimidate Tim to the point that he believed she could prevent him from seeing his daughters, who at the time were five and six years old.

From the way Tim talked at the very first session, it was clear that he was mainly focused on the negative aspects of his wife and his fear of losing his daughters. After an intense three-hour session he understood what he was doing and saw the need to take responsibility and stop accusing others. Once his cowardliness toward his wife and family had been successfully addressed, he henceforth decided to act solely for his own good without blaming others. He quickly understood that in a completely natural way, he could plug himself into another type of current, instead of the negative ones he was used to, and act in conciliatory ways toward his family.

In the weeks that followed, Tim refocused his approach, enjoying himself, being happy and at peace with his daughters, and resisting negative thoughts about his then wife. It's one thing to listen to unpleasant threats, but quite another to engage with them constantly through your thoughts, transforming yourself into a bigger tyrant than "the tyrant." It has nothing to do with being indifferent, vindictive, or cowardly; these behaviors are born from the cold itself, not from the Heart.

In the weeks after our first session, Tim's main task was to pay attention to his thoughts regarding the mother of his daughters. Each time he had a negative thought about her, he would observe his first reaction—the ego is always willing to be the first to judge everything—using an exercise I taught him that I call "centering." He would then instantly and deliberately seek out something in his immediate reality that gave him a boost—anything from rowing to going to the movies to taking the guitar lessons he had recently begun. He voluntarily chose to redirect his thoughts in order to remain connected to the current of well-being.

A couple of months later, grateful and emotional, he told me how his then wife had called him before the divorce hearing to apologize for her behavior, which had been caused by her blind despair and pain. She thanked him for the many times he had tried to calm things down and for the good times they had had as a couple.

Today, three years after the divorce, their relationship remains amicable. Tim not only enjoys the right to visit his young daughters but their mother also allows him to see them whenever he wishes. A deliberate change in focus radically modified Tim's experience—something he couldn't even imagine at first—altering his relationship with this wife and kids for the better.

Like Tim, you too can choose to focus solely on those thoughts that benefit you rather than put down others. You can consciously and deliberately select thoughts that are good, positive, loving, joyful, and conducive to well-being.

Victoria is a good friend. We met in Spain, more than ten years ago, when her life at the time was in turmoil. She was working from home at a company she herself had founded but which did not fulfill her. Her company sold products that assisted people in their quest for a natural and healthy diet. Although she was passionate about the field and the products, she was less so about the work she was engaged in on a daily basis. She was exhausted, disheartened, and did not have the time to enjoy the company of her two children, who were one and five years old at the time. She could not see a way out.

I distinctly recall the look of hope on Victoria's face when, one day over coffee, I asked her if she had ever considered selling the company. She replied that although she had considered it, she did not believe she could earn much from it, given that the company did not hold much promise: she had no website, no contracts with suppliers, no offices, and an almost nonexistent management.

Nonetheless, she asked me to help her in selling the company and in changing her lifestyle, so together we got to work. Victoria focused on her objective on a daily basis: she saw herself selling the company, or having already sold it, and finally enjoying her ideal profession. Determined, she would spend the day consciously and deliberately plugged into luminous currents. In other words, aware of her thoughts and rejecting any that were not good.

After a few days, she contacted a commercial broker who had just opened a branch in her city. Within a month, this brokerage firm succeeded in selling her company to a young executive for the handsome price of half a million dollars.

A few years later, Victoria met the new owner of the company at a trade fair for organic nutrition. They began speaking, and the owner told her that although the company had initially not been in great condition and that it needed a lot of work to yield benefit, the enthusiasm that Victoria had shown when talking about the project and its products had affected him deeply and he had decided to invest in it. In his words: "I felt an intense impulse when I heard your enthusiasm, and I knew the company had to be mine."

I could go on sharing hundreds of examples of people who made important changes by a simple shift in focus, but I think the moment has come to show you the tools that will allow you to enlist the help of your Luminous Being to leave your sleepy state and let go of the automatic pilot that goes hand in hand with your ego when You are not in charge, so you can start creating new experiences of well-being and enrichment.

CHAPTER 19

Ask Your Being

*You are the only creator of and in your life, and it is your duty
to shape the experiences that you wish to live with your Heart.*

We all have the option of consciously directing our thoughts on the one hand or allowing our mind to function freely on automatic pilot on the other. We are like the taxi driver who forgot that he had a passenger with a GPS of Happiness, and as a result carried on driving aimlessly through the streets of the city.

You have the right and the privilege of focusing your mind on new loving and creative thoughts of rich and beneficial experiences—what I call "powerful messages."

Ask Your Being for Everything You Wish to Achieve, Be It Emotional or Material

An empowering message is an order or an assignment that a person issues to the Essence (to the Being, to God Father-Mother) itself. They are neither pleas, nor entreaties, nor supplications, but genuine orders.

This Essence, the offspring of and part of the Essence of the Absolute, is responsible for the good experiences desired by the individual. The Creating Essence of the Absolute, through the principle of co-creation, reproduces all that you ask of it in your life.

It is as if the taxi driver, now aware of the fact that he is carrying a passenger with a GPS of Happiness, were to ask for clear and concrete directions on how to get to the street named "a new nice, lucrative, and fun job," or one called "to enjoy the ideal partner for me," or "total health," or the boulevard of "economic abundance," or "the conscious relationship with my creative Parents," or the road to "a fantastic and conscious rapport with my kids."

The words you utter in these messages are not what is most important; it's the emotion and sensation that accompanies them. Your clear and firm determination is what serves as the impetus behind your message. In other words, the vibrational level from which you utter your order is what will determine the result and what the Essence will perceive your wish to be.

Plug Your Mind Into the Light of Your Heart

In speaking of formulating an empowering message, I do not mean repeating it time and time again with the aim of convincing yourself that it will come to fruition; rather, I mean formulating it from your total consciousness, decision, and willingness.

Imagine for a moment a person looking at herself in the mirror and stating, "I enjoy great economic wealth," but instead of proclaiming it from the totality of her Being and person, saying it simply from her mind. This person, connected as she is to her ego, does not believe what she is saying, nor does she experience the physical sensation that it will be so. Most likely what she will spread instead are sensations of frustration and sadness, albeit subtly. The consequences of this? She will be attracting more experiences in which she will feel precisely those feelings of frustration and sadness.

Repeating messages from a mind that is disconnected from the Heart is akin to the taxi driver, oblivious to his passenger, repeating to himself over and over, "How I wish I could get to the street of joy." Unable to hear his passenger's voice, he will not take the proper route and will never get there, leaving him feeling increasingly powerless, disheartened, and frustrated.

Now imagine two people who buy and read the same book of poetry. One of them recites the poems with intense passion; the other simply reads the poem from the book because he must, without feeling or expressing any emotion whatsoever.

Although the poem is the same, the emotional reaction it provokes in each one is not, nor are the emotions they elicit in those listening. The vibrations sent out by both readers are not the same, just as the vibrations you send out when formulating messages exclusively from your mind are not the same as if you were to do so from the totality of your Being, You, your body, I, the free will within you. The messages must be formulated from a clear and brave free will that chooses to pass through the heart before arriving to the mind and allowing the mouth to speak.

Imagine for a moment a bricklayer who is preparing to build a house. He will need material (body), the know-how (lucidity), commitment, and his decision to actually construct it (free will).

For all the commitment, decisions, and know-how that he may have, he will not be able to construct the house if he lacks the bricks and cement. By the same token, if he had all the requisite material at his disposal but lacked the commitment to work on it every day, or lacked the know-how or the decision, the same problem would arise.

Just as this bricklayer will need these four aspects to build a house, you will need to recognize and apply the four aspects to construct your experiences.

In order to help you formulate messages that are powerful, effective, and in harmony with your well-being, I have created a positioning technique that I call "centering." Be sure to use this technique each time you formulate a new order to your Being, a new empowering message.

The Centering Technique

The aim of this powerful positioning technique is to resume, harmonize, and maintain the contact and communication between your Being (You), your body, and your I—between the taxi driver, the taxi, and the passenger.

The physical gesture adopted in the Centering technique represents the complete communication within you. It is a way to recognize those parts that co-exist in you throughout your daily life: the body and its functions, the telluric energy that nourishes your body, and the Essential energy that illuminates your Heart and serves as a guide to your free will.

STEP 1: Stand in front of a mirror with your knees slightly bent and your legs hip width apart. Look into your eyes.

STEP 2: Place the palm of your right hand on your solar plexus. With this simple gesture, you are signaling to your Being that you acknowledge it and wish and permit it to be present.

STEP 3: Place the palm of your left hand in the center of your chest, over your heart. With this gesture, you are acknowledging your Heart, the Love, and the Light within you.

STEP 4: Focus all your attention consciously and voluntarily on the soles of your feet. The soles of your feet are the gateways of telluric energy. By focusing your attention there, you are telling the Earth, mother of your body, that you recognize its power in it. You are letting the Earth know that you are open and willing to nourish yourself with its energy.

STEP 5: Remain in this position, looking at yourself steadily, with your attention steadfastly fixed on the soles of your feet. In this manner, you will be open to the Essential energy, allowing it to course freely through you, entering the energy center on the crown of your head and flooding your Heart on its path toward the solar plexus.

The Centering technique accesses the most important energy currents: the telluric, which enters through the soles of your feet, and the Essential, which enters through the crown of your head, both of which then meet in the solar plexus, the cradle of your I (free will). Once they meet, they fuse and exit through the solar plexus, expanding in all directions around you.

In the resources section of my website, you will find videos that shows you step-by-step how to perform this and other positioning techniques.

It is important to realize that as you send an empowering message, you emit it from the luminous part of your Being. In the process, you are programming new information throughout your body and transmitting peace and joy to each one of your billions of cells, which work together continuously to nourish and maintain your physical and emotional health.

On my website and on my social network profiles, I offer new and empowering messages daily that I myself formulate to help you, if you need them. It is also important that you remember how to construct your own empowering messages in beneficial ways.

How to Formulate Empowering Messages, Creators of Rich and Good Experiences

Use the following tips to formulate your empowering messages:

FORMULATE YOUR MESSAGES IN THE PRESENT TENSE: The present is the only moment that exists. The past has passed, and the future is something we are now creating. To say, "I am willing to sign off on the sale of my house" is not the same as saying, "In a month's time, I will sign off on the sale of my house." In the second message, you are saying that, in the present moment, you are not going to sign it, that it will always be a month away from the present moment; that is, in a reality that does not exist, and that never will exist.

FORMULATE YOUR MESSAGES IN YOUR FAVOR: There are two powerful reasons to state your message in the positive; that is, emphasizing what you *do* wish to obtain.

The first is that by stating what you don't want—for instance, "not to be in financial straits"—your mind focuses its attention precisely on what you don't want, in this case "financial straits." You then feel the emotions associated with this financial predicament: frustration, anger, and powerlessness, which you continue to experience.

REMEMBER: Emotions, even simple sensations, are more powerful than words.

The second reason is that our minds operate visually. If, for instance, I say to you, "Don't think of apples!" Isn't the first thing you thought of apples, and lots of them? Make sure that the words or thoughts you offer your mind are ones that will create an image of what you do wish to enjoy in your life, so that it instantly sees the desired situation and triggers the pleasurable emotions associated with this already attained situation. In this way, you will be creating a reality more favorable to you. Instead of saying, "I no longer live in this small house," you can say, "I allow myself to live in a nice house with X number of bedrooms, a garden, and so on."

BE AS SPECIFIC AS POSSIBLE: Before formulating an empowering message, it is important to clarify as much as possible what it is you wish to create.

I remember a good friend of mine who spent four years trying to sell three feature-length screenplays in Hollywood. Following a brief discussion about empowering messages and how to use them, she began working on the next message, "I sign the contract for my first screenplay."

Within a month, she had sold her first screenplay. We agreed to meet the same day to celebrate, but contrary to what one might have expected, my friend was sad and frustrated. She explained that the reason for her frustration was that she had thought they would pay her much more for the screenplay. She had focused on selling her screenplay and not on what she wished to obtain from the sale of it. She had not specified exactly what she wanted.

Following this conversation, she modified her message to, "I sell my screenplay quickly, easily, and to my best financial advantage." Within six months she had sold her second screenplay, and this time at an even higher price than she expected.

BE CONCISE: The more concise the messages are the clearer they will be, and therefore the more power they will have. Look at the difference: "I'm totally open to enjoy my new ideal job" or "I'm doing the interview for that job I found the other day in the newspaper for X company offering a salary of Y." In the second example the mind loses itself in details, thereby diluting the emotion that we are looking to create and strengthen.

FORMULATE MESSAGES YOU CAN IDENTIFY WITH, WHICH SOUND REAL AND POSSIBLE: A person who is overweight and says "I have a slender body" will not believe it. The discrepancy with reality will make him feel frustrated, thereby sending out a vibration that will keep him at the same weight. It would be better if he said something like, "I am in the process of getting back to my ideal weight" or "I'm recovering my ideal weight."

If what you are affirming doesn't seem real to you, if you cannot feel it as a fact that already exists, you can try the following phrases:

I am in the process of obtaining my ideal _____ .

I authorize myself to enjoy my ideal _____ .

I permit myself to enjoy my ideal _____ .

INCLUDE AT LEAST ONE DYNAMIC FEELING OR A WORD RELATED TO FEELINGS: In formulating your messages, include words that describe the emotion you would like to experience when reaching your goal. "I enjoy socializing with new ideal friends for me." "What a joy being able to celebrate the sale of my first book." "I am delighted to see my earnings grow daily." "I feel happy and delighted to share… " and so on.

Some words or expressions that are particularly effective are: *accept, enjoy, triumph, it delights me, I'm enthusiastic about, I am happy about, it thrills me, I'm passionate about, I celebrate, I feel happy, joyful, calm, soothed, enthusiastic, loving, secure, serene*, and so on.

FORMULATE THE MESSAGES EXCLUSIVELY FOR AND FROM YOURSELF: Just as you cannot create anything in someone else's life, you cannot formulate messages for anybody but yourself. If, for instance, you have a poor relationship with one of your children, you can say: "I strengthen the harmony in my relationship with Jane" instead of saying, "I wish my daughter would change."

I often receive emails from people asking me what they can do to make another person fall in love with them, or to make someone around them change. There is nothing you can do to make someone else fall in love with you; it simply doesn't work that way. Nevertheless, you do have the power to create a reality that you can enjoy with a person with whom you feel happy, loved, and loving. By the same token, you cannot make someone else change; you can only make appropriate changes in order to stop obsessing about this person, or stop giving this person so much importance that it causes you, and the other person, pain.

CHOOSE TO STOP PLACING LIMITS ON YOUR HAPPINESS: Let's take situations in which you are ordering something specific: living in a certain place, driving a specific car, living in a particular house, or receiving a specific sum of money. Who knows? Perhaps we are issuing these orders from our limited human mind and closing ourselves off to even better, or much better, opportunities.

Imagine, for example, that you have spent your holidays in a fantastic place to which you would like to move but have not figured out how. So, you say something like, "I'm willing to move to Washington D.C." But perhaps D.C. is not the ideal place for you, based on the knowledge of your Being, therefore you could add, "I enjoy living in Washington D.C. or in a place even better suited to me." On the one hand, you maintain the emotion, the pleasurable sensation of making a change for living in that place, while at the same time giving free rein to the Essence of your Being to create an even better experience in which this pleasant sensation can be even more intense.

AVOID USING THE WORDS "WANT" OR "DESIRE" AT THE START OF YOUR MESSAGES: "Want" implies that something is lacking. Saying "want" is equivalent to saying, "I don't have." Remember to formulate your messages as genuine orders. Instead of "I want to live in a new house," you can say, "I accept to enjoy living in the house of my dreams" or "What I do want is …"

FOCUS ON ONE THING IN EACH MESSAGE: If you fail to focus on one thing in each message, the energy will be dispersed. Imagine you formulate your order in this way, "I enjoy living in my ideal home, with a safe car, next to the partner of my dreams." Your mind first sees the house, followed by the car, then the partner of your dreams. But what is the main sensation? Your dispersed thoughts can't construct a clear emotion. The message you issue is like driving on a highway through different towns and the radio can't pick up any signal clearly.

HOW AND WHEN TO ISSUE ORDERS TO YOUR BEING: You can formulate your orders whenever you wish throughout the day, but it is important and effective to begin your day with a vibration creating well-being. Therefore, once you've gotten ready for the day, give yourself a few minutes, stand in front of a mirror in the centering position, and using your empowering messages, allow yourself to communicate with the energy currents most beneficial to you.

A good thing to do is to reinforce this creating vibration several times throughout your day. Reformulate your messages whenever you wish to or are able to. If your daily activity does not allow you to repeat the centering routine, at least try to formulate your messages while looking in the mirror.

Keep in mind the importance of the universal principles at your disposal, consciously choosing your thoughts and connecting yourself to the creating currents of well-being. Once you remember how to issue orders to your Being, you will also need to remember how to soothe your ego and handle your emotions.

CHAPTER 20

When the Ego Attacks

Your ego needs you to put limits on it; it needs you to show presence and security.

Oftentimes, when we've embarked on a change in our daily lives, our ego will become particularly active in trying to discourage us, making us believe that everything is pointless, that nothing is worth the effort or that you, regardless of how much you try, will never achieve what you've set out to do, or that it's all too complicated, difficult, or even boring.

Granted, making changes requires practice, consistency, and, above all else, a lot of Self-Love. It also took you time to learn something as simple and natural as walking or talking. How many years did you spend in the education system before obtaining the degree you have today?

In this material and spatial experience you are living, you need time to learn, or in this case, to rediscover things. Once you understand the undeniable benefits of reclaiming your path in Love and Happiness, you'll realize it's a worthwhile effort, especially if your priority is to start to exist, to feel the Happiness flowing through your life like blood coursing through your veins, and not just functioning or surviving.

What takes greater effort? Remaining in your ignorance and suffering, day after day, with its painful consequences, such as lack of money, poor health, sadness, bad relationships, solitude, lack of motivation, distress, anxiety, dissatisfaction in the workplace, fear, apathy, and so forth? Or returning to You and authorizing yourself to enjoy the infinite and gratifying joy of existing and in the process, constructing the fulfilling life you promised yourself you would live?

The Ego's Resistance to Your Changes

Your ego, like everyone else's, fears change and tends to resist it. Accustomed to being in charge and directing the course of your life, it feels suddenly threatened and scared. In a way, it is afraid it will disappear. It is just like a spoiled child who becomes afraid at the sudden appearance of limits and rules. At the beginning of this new education, it does not understand what is happening. Confused and anxious, it tries to make more noise so that you don't forget it's there. Just as you would soothe a scared or rebellious child, you can do the same with your ego. It only needs for you to soothe it, needs for you to show it your security.

Learn to Quiet Down Your Ego

The moment you feel any kind of emotional distress or catch yourself having negative thoughts or unpleasant sensations, it's a sign your ego is the one holding the reins of your experiences. All you need to do is soothe it, put it in its place, place limits, and show it your Presence and security.

To connect with your ego and soothe it, visualize it as a child manifesting itself in all of its negative modes: the cruel child, the rebellious child, the unruly child, the child who talks back, the malicious child, the vengeful child, the bored child, and so forth. Speak to it as the adult you are.

In situations in which it is scared, kneel to its level, saying, "Shhh. This is none of your affair. I'm here. I'm in charge. Everything is alright."

In situations in which it is trying to drive you into misdeeds, say, "Shhh. I'm in charge here."

Imagine you have a six-year-old kid in front of you who says, "Mommy, Mommy, what if we don't have anything to eat tomorrow?"

What would you do? Surely you wouldn't be drawn into his fear and respond, "Oh dear, that's true. How horrible. I don't know what we're going to do." You would calm her down, telling her that it's not her business, that you're in charge, and of course, that it's something you and only you can deal with. You would say something like, "Don't worry, sweetie. I'm here to take care of this" or "That's something I take care of." Wouldn't you?

Now imagine the case of a child who was trying to control your life by saying things like, "I want chocolate ice cream (right before dinner)," "I don't want to brush my teeth," "I don't want to go visit Granny," "I want the car that so-and-so's mother has," "I'll do that tomorrow," "I only want to eat pasta, or French fries, or such-and-such a hamburger, and a soda. Even though this is junk food, I like it!" "I want the neighbor's video game," and so on.

What would you do? Are you one of those who would act according to the child's will, or would you play the role of adult and true caregiver and educate the child by setting the limits that will help her to understand her mistakes by herself?

The Quest for Limits

Children need to be educated, to grow in a safe environment, and to feel loved and safe. Every one of their negative behaviors is a warning, often a cry of despair for the adult to come and help her, or about testing limits.

I'm sure you've heard of the "terrible twos." This is the period when two-year-olds experiment with all types of things and play all kinds of pranks, looking to us to teach them what they may or may not do. Limits provide them with security and offer them a framework in which they can grow and develop in security.

In order to develop in harmony and well-being, children need to feel that their educators are setting boundaries that are stable and consistent, loving but firm. They need to feel that they are there to accompany and protect them; in other words, to educate them and help them grow—not suffocate them. In this way, children get familiar with the path on Earth that fosters well-being, thereby liberating their Happiness and allowing their Growth. Although this is not always the result of education, it remains its constant aim.

This is precisely what our ego expects of us. It seeks affection, limits, security, and the feeling that it can trust us. Only in this way can it be transformed, and it knows it.

What would happen if we educated children without offering them these limits?

Imagine a two-year-old child who starts making mischief and does not receive guidance about what is or is not acceptable behavior. Confused and without limits, he tries to push the envelope a little farther, with the aim of understanding what he can or can't do. He tests his educators and his environment in search of defined limits, his references for life.

If he is unable to find the limits he needs, his anxiety, confusion, and sense of danger grow, as a result of his not being able to distinguish which actions are risky and which are not. Without limits, he feels the anguish of not knowing where to turn, he feels apathy and lack of satisfaction in his actions, as he doesn't know whether he is going to be recognized and rewarded systematically or randomly punished.

This is exactly what happens with our ego. It seeks limits and looks to us to assume our role soothing it and offering it security; in other words, mature and grow as human beings. When our ego addresses us, we tend to listen and believe what it says without even realizing who is talking. We let ourselves be carried away by its dark emotion, or we ignore it and think of other things, or even get angry at it for being there, for existing in us, often berating and criticizing, and even threatening, ourselves.

Offer It Your Security and Your Loving Presence

The only thing your ego needs is to see that it can trust you. When you demonstrate that you are present, that you are solid and there for yourself and for it, then and only then does it quiet down. Its voice is then lulled to sleep, allowing the voice of your Heart to take over. Show it that whatever happens, You have the situation in hand, that You are in charge, that You are there to calm it down and allow Happiness to flow independently of what may happen or of what it may say to you.

Joe was a young man who suffered from frequent and sudden panic attacks. In spite of spending several months on strong medication his problem only seemed to worsen. He came to see me after having listened to a presentation I had given at the company he works for.

Joe realized quickly that in spite of having achieved great professional success, he felt an intense fear of losing it all. When I asked him if there was any basis for this fear, he said that no, there was nothing in his reality that justified his thinking in this way, but that there was what he referred to as "that horrible voice" inside that would not leave him in peace. Joe tried desperately to silence it by staying busy, doing a thousand different things in order not to hear it, but only succeeded in making the voice stronger.

In the course of our first session, Joe became aware of the catastrophic messages that his ego, given free rein, was relentlessly throwing at him: "You're going to end up with nothing," "One day you're going to lose it all," "Life is unjust," "What if you're in an accident and end up paralyzed, or die?", "You don't deserve everything you have," "Your wife is too good for you," "And what if she dies and you're left alone?", and so on.

I suggested that he try to visualize his ego as a little child who was very scared and who simply wanted to be reassured. After hours of intense work, he was able to have a new way of looking at the little internal voice that had seemed to him so ferocious. Soon, he was able to wean himself off his medication and from what he told me, to this day he has had no further relapses.

I'm in Charge Here

Jennifer had just completed her university studies when she came to see me. She felt sad and alone since all the girls of her age had good friends or partners and she had no one. She said that she could not seem to maintain any of her friendships since her friends all ended up distancing themselves from her for no apparent reason. They would simply stop calling or become estranged and she would not hear from them again. Jennifer desperately longed to be important to another person.

When speaking of her former friends, she did so with rancor, criticism, and resentment. After listening to several long tirades from her darkest inner self, she realized from where she had been speaking all along. I helped her to see how her ego manipulated her as a rebellious and sulking child who always looks for the flaws in others. It quickly dawned on her that she had been the one to push away her friends through her critical, superior, and somewhat mocking behavior. She also discovered that her ego was feeding her harsh and critical messages because it felt frightened and inferior to others.

The moment Jennifer resorted to her Heart and lucidity, she took back command of the ship, as it were, and as a result of reclaiming power over herself inwardly and soothing her ego, she gradually began to feel better.

She realized that, actually, this behavior was something she had been copying from her father, that it did not belong to her, that she was mimicking it in order to feel recognized by this critical and insecure man who constantly looked for faults in others, and especially in his own daughter. Leaving her first session, one of her old friends had sent her a message asking her how she was and congratulating her on her graduation. It seemed incredible to her.

The moment Jenny managed to pacify her ego and regain her power using her Heart, she immediately plugged herself into a new energy current of affection and authenticity toward herself, a current where friendship existed and from which she could share her reclaimed Heart with her former friend.

REMEMBER: Every time you feel a negative emotion or any kind of distress, stop and identify the thoughts that are causing this dark sensation or emotion. Identify the message that your ego is trying to transmit to you and pacify it. Offer it your caring presence, resolve, decisiveness, steadiness, and peace. Let it know that it can trust You.

CHAPTER 21

Your Emotions Are
Your Best Indicator

*Tell me what you feel, and I'll tell you
what you are creating.*

Through the universal principle of co-creation, you have the irrevocable power to create your life based on the currents to which you connect yourself by way of your thoughts and emotions. But how do you know which one you are giving more importance to: the ego or the Heart?

Your emotions indicate which type of energy current you are plugging yourself into. Each time you feel a pleasant emotion, it is a sign that you are plugged into a luminous current of Love and thereby creating a life of well-being. On the contrary, each time you feel a painful emotion or you're bored or you don't feel any type of emotion at all, it is a sign that your are plugged into a negative current and thereby bringing suffering into your life.

It is really as simple as that. Every time you feel good, you are expanding Love; every time you feel bad, you are expanding darkness.

In this dark universe, there are two primordial emotions: Love and fear. All other emotions we feel are variations and derivations of these. Not feeling anything is also a choice made from darkness. The person who doesn't feel is devoid of Love, and this hole, this void, will invariably be filled by absence and directed by fear.

You can picture your interior as a dark room without windows, the door closed and the lights off. All you have to do is turn on the light switch for light to flood the darkness. The choice is yours.

You probably have heard the expression "Waking up on the wrong side of the bed." This expression refers to the principle of co-creation and how we attract situations based on how we feel. If we wake up in a bad mood, feeling sad or powerless, and remain in this mood, we are already connecting ourselves to dark currents. If we then do nothing to remedy the situation, we often end up having a disastrous day, filled with distress. But if our day gets off "on the right foot"—or even "the wrong foot" but we correct it—the rest of the day is often just as pleasant as that wonderful awakening.

Your Ego Needs Care

The ego is accustomed to thinking incessantly and dominating the internal conversation, without being silenced or pacified; as a result, it is constantly proposing negative thoughts to you. These negative thoughts, which we are mostly not even aware of, will trigger in us a large spectrum of dark and therefore painful emotions.

The problem is that in most cases, we don't even realize that the ego is talking to us. According to various scientific studies, 96 percent of our actions are driven by thoughts and feelings that are beyond our conscious awareness. Given that we have between fifty and sixty thousand thoughts a day, and the majority are fed to us by our ego, it is clearly impossible to control them all. It is much easier and effective to learn to pay attention to our emotions and choose to strengthen the thoughts that speak to us of things that are actually important to us, in the here and now, and that relate to the Heart.

When perceiving the least bit of emotional distress, a person who is centered and in constant communication with her Being and mindful of her Heart will ask herself, "What is causing this sensation?" From within her awakened Being, she readily understands what's happening and can then subdue her ego. When this ego feels listened to and understood, it is easily pacified and gradually grows calmer and quieter. As a result, this person feels increasingly free from negative emotions and as a result, she is happier.

It is of utmost importance to recognize the presence of your ego in your mind or your words as the means to stop its negative messages, re-educate it, and soothe it.

When the ego proposes its dark ideas to us, which in most cases don't even reach our conscious awareness, we feel bad and simply resist, try to ignore them, or let ourselves be drawn into a thousand things to do. We rarely decide to understand where the distress is coming from.

Learn to Deal with Dark Emotions

When experiencing an unpleasant emotion, most people tend to do one of three things: resist it, attempt to ignore it, or be drawn into it and submerged by suffering. In any one of these cases, the result is a heavy dose of distress.

Do you remember what we were discussing earlier about the roles that people adopt? What would a person do who principally plays the role of the tyrant? Without doubt, any time this person feels bad she will make others pay for it, with aggression, accusation, or other kinds of abuse.

What about a victim? He will possibly spend the day submerged in his emotions, ruminating and complaining about the unhappiness that others or life itself has caused him.

And the hyper-rational? Well, assuming she is able to feel something to begin with, she will try to ignore it, escape, or do something to once again avoid feeling it in order to return to her monotonous and empty life devoid of emotion and teeming with reason.

REMEMBER: You cannot heal your darkness using its own ruses. The only thing you can do is to take back your Peace using the tools of your Heart.

Imagine three friends who have just arrived in New York. Thrilled because it's their first visit to the Big Apple, they ask a stranger for directions on how to get to the infamous Central Park. The man tells them that all they have to do is continue walking down the same road.

The three friends, with growing enthusiasm, walk in the direction indicated by the man. Soon, they think, they will get to the park so many people talk about and which they have long wanted to explore. Then, to their dismay, the road they're on suddenly ends in front of a high brick wall.

Disconcerted, they don't know what to do next. One of them, feeling cheated and angry, hits the wall with all his might, but of course, walls generally don't move just because someone decides that they shouldn't be there. The more he strikes the wall and hurls insults at the man whom he now deems malicious for having tricked them, the more frustrated, powerless, and furious he feels.

One of his friends sits down and leans his back against the unexpected obstacle. Sitting thus, he curses his bad luck for how unhappy he feels, for how harshly life has treated him, and for once again nothing having turned out the way he'd hoped.

The third man, seeing the spectacle his friends are putting on, takes out his Smartphone and begins to read his messages, go onto social networks, and play a video game. He tries to escape the situation with every means at his disposal.

In none of the three cases—the one who resists, the one who is immersed in pain, and the one who evades the issue—has the obstacle been overcome and the desired goal achieved: taking a walk in the park.

Alternatively, they could have accepted that the wall existed and represented a perfectly surmountable obstacle, and this would have helped to alleviate their feelings of powerlessness, allowed them to reorient themselves, and thereby get to the park. This is what happens with our undesired emotions; only accepting them and making a firm decision to find a solution can help us overcome them.

Resisting an obstacle only leads to frustration—the obstacle remains an obstacle, and as such, will not budge; instead, you have to be the one to change course.

Imagine that you are walking through your house and run into a piece of furniture. What do you do? Are you going to resist it by pushing against it or simply walk around it and carry on? Painful emotions are akin to these obstacles in your path. They have a solution!

Every time you are invaded by a painful emotion, stop, recognize it, find its source, and make the decision to release it. Decide (which requires a change) that you have no interest in remaining in this pain and suffering that it provokes in you.

Decide to Let Go of Painful Emotions

When faced with any kind of unwanted emotion, talk to your ego and pacify it in the manner I've illustrated to you.

Sometimes, however, the ego has taken up so much space for so long, it is difficult to get it to quiet down. For moments like these, I have created a technique that I call "Breathe It Out." This technique, used by my students for more than two decades, is a very effective way to release stagnant emotions, tensions, and dry tears and regain the vitality that is always sapped by darkness.

Prior to employing this technique, take a moment to identify precisely what it is that you want to free yourself from. To do that, you will have to identify the cause of your distress. Perhaps it was a comment, a thought, a criticism, a disparaging remark, a verbal or physical attack, a belief, some unexpected and unpleasant situation (your partner leaves you, you lose your job), and so forth. Situations like these may be the cause of distressing sensations or emotions, but you can free yourself from them by employing the "Breathe It Out" technique.

Once you've identified what you want to liberate yourself from, keep it firmly in mind while applying the technique. Free your space as if you wanted to hurl this darkness out of your inner self, out of your vehicle, as if you wanted to throw out that wasp that has entered when you carelessly left the window open.

This exercise, far from being an escape or a struggle, allows you to confront the emotion, recognize it in order to release it, and leave a new space for the love to expand and for its light to shine again.

Stand with your knees slightly bent, your legs a few centimeters apart. Now begin to slowly raise your arms with your palms facing up, as though you are reaching for "that something that bothers you" above your head. Breathe in deeply as you do this, and keep your attention firmly on the soles of your feet.

Once your hands are above your head, with your arms completely stretched, make the gesture of reaching up to grasp whatever is disturbing you, be it a sensation, a thought, a behavior, a memory, or some situation that you do not desire in your life. Close your hands, as if holding the distress in them, tighten your hands into fists, then firmly lower your arms back down to the sides, bending your elbows so that your fists remain close to your body. Now you're in charge. When your arms are at waist height make a quick releasing movement with your hands as if you wanted to throw what you had in your hands down toward the Earth.

While you lower your arms, exhale while making the sound *fooaahh*, lengthening the final vowel. Feel the sound and the exhalation coming directly from your solar plexus. Make sure you don't scream from your throat but let the air out from your stomach.

Repeat this movement as many times as you feel you need to, until you feel completely free from the emotion or sensation that is causing you distress.

With each *fooaahh*, eject the darkness from inside you and say, "Out." Free yourself, release as much as you need, with anger if necessary, with the determination that this is what you want. Note that when I say do it with anger, I don't mean anger toward something, someone, or your ego but the liberating anger that accompanies the feeling of "That's enough now!"—in other words, the mature decision to stop causing yourself any harm.

In the resources section of my website, you will find explanatory videos on how to perform this technique.

Illuminate Your Space

Once you have liberated your fear and stress, you will have automatically recovered your inner space. You will feel that you have returned to the Peace of your Heart and your interior silence, seemingly untouched by the mind or the ego.

Once you have freed yourself from the tensions created by harmful emotions, allow yourself to fill in the new space with loving thoughts that will create emotions of Happiness for you. Look at yourself in the mirror and, using the "centering" position, formulate powerful messages such as the ones I outlined earlier.

One useful message for a moment like this is, "I am Love, and I declare the Joy in me." You will instantly and naturally feel filled with new and gratifying currents of well-being.

If the situation allows it, when you've completed this process of liberation, take a few minutes to focus on relaxation. Lie down on a firm mat, and make sure that your body is comfortable; that is, that you're neither cold nor hot, that you don't have tension in your body, that you don't need to use the restroom, and so on. Listen to some relaxing music, or simply lie in silence with your right palm on your solar plexus and your left palm on your heart. Your attention, as always, should be on your feet. Remain in this meditative state of relaxation for a few minutes before getting up slowly and gently.

The Liberating Cry

If at any moment during this exercise, or at any moment during your day, you feel like crying, let yourself do so. Crying helps release heavy accumulated tension and emotion. Cry in order to let it go, to both free and forgive yourself. As you allow the crying to cleanse and liberate you, from within your Being say, "I forgive you (your name). Yes, I do love you," and calmly respond to your Being by saying, "Thank you. I also love myself and choose to forgive myself."

It is vital that you differentiate between crying to let go—to free and forgive yourself, allowing Love and Peace and openness to flow through your entire body—and the crying of victimization and lamentation to which people are so accustomed.

Any time you feel the need to cry, ask yourself: "Where is this need coming from? From the feeling of 'Woe is me," 'Look at what's happening to me,' 'Look at what I've done,' 'Why me?', or from the desire to free and forgive myself for my human errors and forgive others for theirs?" Crying as the victim lamenting his fate only serves to deepen the darkness and amplify this painful emotion in you, and it may also affect those around you.

Crying to let go, on the other hand, is an act of love that helps you to continue your evolutionary path while freeing yourself from the low energy vibration and allowing Love to course through your inner space. This permits you to raise the energy level and get plugged into energy currents of greater well-being.

The "Breathe It Out" technique, although ideal in itself, is not always practical in every situation in our daily lives. There will be moments when it is simply not possible to apply it. Sometimes, my students and I laugh when they tell me about their adventures and anecdotes concerning times in which they've tried to apply this technique in public places or in the workplace. There are companies that have incorporated it into their workday, so that all employees have a few minutes to release their tensions before starting work.

In cases in which it is impossible to perform this exercise, speak to your ego immediately and clearly. Calm it down until you can find an appropriate time and place for releasing whatever it is that bothers you. Each time your ego fails to meet with resistance, evasion, or eruptions of anger, but instead finds awareness and firm direction, it will continue to abate and weaken.

The Three Great Hindrances to Happiness

There are three emotions that will become obstacles to your Happiness if you include them in your life: fear, permanent sadness, and rancor, or indifference, the other side of which is guilt.

CHAPTER 22

Heal Your Fear

Just as human beings are born with their own sense of guilt, fear is also inherent in them. The Being, as we have seen, is Light crossing through darkness, and given that the emotional manifestation of darkness is fear, people are already born with fear inside.

Moreover, this fear, which is innate to us all, is reinforced by our forgetting of Who we are, and Who our Parents are.

Consider for a moment a person who is born and cannot remember who he is or what he is doing here. What else can he feel but a sense of panic? He sees himself inhabiting a planet that, in his eyes, is immense and floating in the midst of a great dark void. Nothing is holding this planet up. And as if this weren't enough, he discovers that this planet on which he walks is spinning in space at a vertiginous rate. There are millions of asteroids passing close by the Earth and at any time one of them could well strike it. And what do you make of the moon that spends its time revolving on its own axis, without anything to keep it from falling on us or pulling the Earth out of its orbit?

To the human senses and perception, this reality produces a sense of vertigo, it produces genuine terror. The human being feels alone, on a planet that floats, surrounded by millions of dangers, in the middle of an immense, cold and dark space.

Self-Deception

The only thing that this person knows, asleep from her Knowledge, is what other humans teach her or what she experiences by means of her limited sense perception. In fact, she avoids thinking about it altogether. If she had to live with the knowledge that she has no idea why she is on this planet, who or what she really is, where she came from or where she is headed, it would be too unbearable for her reason to deal with.

People live their lives knowing that they are tricking themselves in order to survive, believing that they have no control whatsoever over their experience. The fact that they see everyone else just as confused and lost as they are encourages them to continue living, surviving, behaving like others, at least in order not to feel alone in their Ignorance of Who they are. At one point or another, most people have asked themselves these same questions and have arrived at the same conclusions, "If others do it, or don't do it, I will or won't do it, too."

Away from our Light, blinded to our Knowledge, we elect to copy others, to imitate and do what it appears we are supposed to do. We decide to live like others and stop asking ourselves questions which, given that we cannot understand them with our mind, lead us nowhere. So, what's the point in keeping thinking about the meaning of my Life?

It's clear now why so many people are afraid of dying.

At the end of their lives, the questions they decided to set aside and forget begin once more to surface—questions that were left unanswered in order to survive on this planet, yet with the hope that one day someone might illuminate them on their path, that someone might respond for them.

For the majority of people, however, the day comes, and these questions remain an immense unknown. An unknown that produces dread. For most, these questions will remain unanswered until the day they abandon their material bodies.

Fear is a constant in the life of human beings. It is only when we re-establish contact with our Being that we can regain the security and peace of knowing that we are one with the Essence itself, that we are safe, loved, and supported in each moment by Love Father-Mother.

Fear of the Unknown

The human being is fearful of the unknown, especially when faced with that which he cannot perceive with the conventional human senses.

The limited human senses are adapted to what the human mind-ego, unaware of the Being, can withstand. If human beings could see and perceive Reality and interpret it only by way of the mind, they would not be able to withstand it and would go insane or die of panic. Imagine you could see the different planes that inhabit the same space as you inhabit and that you could see how other beings pass through your physical body. Without a doubt, the fear it would trigger would be intense, and if it were constantly like this, do you think you could withstand it? No. Exclusively from your mind, you could not.

Nevertheless, although you cannot see or perceive the Reality in which you live in its totality, you can sense, because you know it from within your

Being, that there is a lot more to it than your mind-ego and your senses are telling you. This perception, or knowing without actually seeing, has created a lot of fear and incomprehension over the course of humanity's entire history.

The Fear of "Ghosts"

One of the fears that my students most often speak to me of in the privacy of our sessions is the fear of what you would call "ghosts." Let's try to shed some sense and clarity on this chaos and incomprehension regarding the "atomic bodies" of beings who have abandoned their human bodies, or, as you usually refer to it, have died.

Our Beings arrive on this planet with a specific capital of Light surrounded by a certain quantity of darkness, with the sole aim of continuing to evolve; this is to say, to expand their Light thus diminishing darkness without resorting to a fight. The degree to which a Being has increased its Light, its luminous capital, will determine its subsequent experience as a Being; in other words, it will determine the continuation of its journey.

Do you remember the energy currents that we plug ourselves into? Well, on a much larger scale, this occurs across the entire universe. There are currents and places of differing levels of luminosity or darkness. There are places that are much more luminous than the dense material planet on which we currently live, just as there are even darker places. Thanks to the Heart and the Beauty of our Parents—of Creation itself—most places are more luminous than Earth.

Once your Being leaves its material body and prepares to continue its path, it will use its luminous capital as fuel to travel, or simply move to other places. The light you will have generated in this experience is that which will determine which places you will or will not be able to travel or move to.

In many, if not most cases, the human, ignorant of his Being, his Reality, and therefore mainly mindful of his ego, will not increase his light and will do little to enhance his luminous capital during his earthly experience.

Given that the atomic body does not possess enough Light to travel to a more luminous, and therefore happier place, it has different options. It can always incarnate itself into another human body and "repeat the grade," or it can decide that it no longer wishes to incarnate itself as a human and remains on Earth with its atomic body, without a material body, with the additional aim of increasing its Light and thus being able to continue on its path later on.

Since in the latter case, the physical body, a product of matter, is abandoned, the same spatial-temporal principles do not apply, and these Beings, in their atomic state, can remain in that state for what to us may seem like milliseconds, centuries, or millennia. Divested of their limiting human and material bodies, they can be in several places at once or travel instantaneously from one place to another.

Those atomic bodies, devoid of a physical body, are what humans call "ghosts." Naturally, they have nothing to do with the feared ghosts that film, literature, or popular culture depict. Their intention is not to harm anybody; just the opposite—in this state, they are perfectly aware of the errors they do not wish to repeat. The natural process of Life will help them to continue on their adventure through mysterious and exciting Eternity.

The Atomic Body of Our Ancestors

One of the reasons that human beings and popular culture fear these atomic bodies, these "ghosts," or Beings that have not yet departed, is simply that most (not all) of the world's population remains immersed in ignorance regarding this issue.

From our very first years, it is important for us to be able to speak about what we call "death" without taboos or negative mysteries. On the other hand, just like you, your biological parents imitated the behaviors of their biological parents, who did the same with their biological parents, and so on. The dark behaviors that you had promised yourself you wouldn't repeat in this life are, therefore, the same as those of your ancestors, not yet departed, now trying to liberate themselves with the help of Love.

When you are more in your ego, you may feel that your ancestors are closer. You may feel that they are still in your space, or you may simply be obsessed with some issue that you haven't finished resolving with them, and you might then feel goosebumps or fear. But invariably, and without realizing it, in this way you connect to their vibrations and darkness, thereby increasing it even more in you.

Just as you chose to be a master to your biological parents by not copying their negative behaviors, you can also be one to your ancestors, to a point. Severing the dark current that connects you by changing direction and stopping feeding the darkness that your human family has shared for generations is something you can do to liberate yourself first; you can then work to liberate your ancestors. I'm not saying that you have to save them, nor that their trajectory in the hereafter depends on you freeing yourself from atavisms and negative behaviors repeated generation after generation. No. But it's always better to "not stoke the fire."

Your Adventure through eternity is about Love.

For example, if you see in your family that nobody ever paid attention to anyone, or nobody hugged anybody, or nobody spoke about Love, and showing it was an even greater taboo, stop stoking the flames that burn us instead of creating Light. The ancestors who languish in darkness have no intention of harming you; in fact, they can do nothing to you, because they have no material body. They can, however, influence you every time you use those bad intentions or thoughts or decisions that you still share with them daily without even realizing it.

In a following chapter, when we speak in depth of death and what it represents, I will offer you some examples of my beautiful experiences with Beings which, once they have abandoned their material bodies, have chosen to remain on this planet as atomic bodies while naturally increasing their luminous-love capital.

Love, Then You Will Heal Your Fear

In life, you've probably seen often that Light has more power than darkness, and that light is Light only when it is an expression of Love. Right?

As much as Hollywood may cast doubt on the matter, Light is always Loving-Creative, and not destructive.

Choose to be aware of your Heart by learning from its Knowledge and enjoying its light, because without even realizing it, you will be plugging yourself into an energy current that will only serve to bring you more Happiness and rich and pleasant experiences.

Darkness that is bathed by your present and growing Light, thanks to your new thoughts and decisions, will surround you but not invade you. It will not be able to enter and steal your lucidity, nor manipulate your functions or senses.

In general, thieves only break into empty homes. They think twice when you're home.

Cast Away the Sadness in Your Life

Sadness is the opposite of action.

Sadness is one of the many emotional manifestations of fear, and for that reason, it is an emotion intrinsic to the human being. Sadness arises from the lack of acceptance of the process of Life. But how are we to accept the natural process of Life if we don't understand What we are doing here, Who we are, or What our mission is? How can we accept the process of Life if we don't even accept ourselves? How can we accept it if we have made of death our most feared and inexorable enemy?

The fear that arises from forgetting Who we are when we're born on this planet, provokes in people the need to control everything, an anxious and mistaken need for security. Nobody can control Life and its natural processes, even if we try to do so through the demand of our egos.

Speaking of death, we will only be able to accept it with the help of the Knowledge that lies within our Heart. If we are not aware of this fact, we will feel powerless every time there's a new death in our life.

And what can come of powerlessness but great anger and a feeling of complete injustice, which often leads us to accuse God Himself. Sadness arises from that mistaken and immature feeling regarding God Father-Mother. This feeling is the opposite of taking responsibility, or accepting the natural process of Life. It is the opposite of action, and in certain cases, of humility.

REMEMBER: Light is an expression of Love. It is speed, it is movement. Immobility, passivity, resentment, and powerlessness are characteristic of ignorance.

The Loss of a Loved One

It is perfectly understandable, given the way we are educated, that the loss of a loved one provokes a temporary sadness in you, simply because the person with whom you've shared so many moments of your life on Earth is someone you (think you) will never see again. The problem arises when the person, despite time having passed after the loss, remains in this state of sadness, blindly and apathetically locked in this sadness, without realizing that he is using it to continue to cry and feel pity for himself.

You would be surprised at the number of people who wait for these events, either personally or not, to give themselves an excuse to be able to cry about their own selves and realities without anybody judging them.

Having said that, people have very different ways of reacting to the loss of a loved one. Some people come to have sessions with me after months of depression, feeling devastated and convinced that there's no way out. They say death can't be overcome, as they hadn't chosen it nor wanted it and believe there's nothing afterwards, or even worse, afterwards they only see hell as a possibility for them.

Others come ready to carry on with their lives immediately, even when the loss is recent and very painful. Some people have even met a new significant other or even gotten pregnant again to not feel the void, to not feel alone.

The truth is that everyone is free and has the power to choose how to react in each moment of their lives.

It is easy to understand why people who are still ignorant of the workings of Life (despite all the higher education they may have received) suffer indescribably when facing the death of a loved one. To the solely rational human mind, death is an inexplicable and moreover, completely unacceptable. Isn't the death of a loved one a silent echo of our own Internal Knowledge that we are eternal?

For the person, asleep to his eternal Reality, it is simply the most terrifying and frightening thing, because they don't know when or how it will happen. He cannot control it, much less avoid it!

Seeing a loved one die, people are forced to remember the very thing they prefer not to think about in their day-to-day life: that at any moment, a loved one or they themselves may die. And this thought terrifies them.

Will I ever see this departed person again or is this the end? This painful thought creates suffering and anger, and great resentment—resentment against Creation itself. For most of the world's population, the fact of dying creates a sense of utter incomprehension and injustice.

Many people ask themselves: "How can one live happily if at any moment 'the worst' might happen?"

It takes some time to make an earthly mother or father see that death is nothing more than the continuation of our path as eternal Beings, especially when they have forgotten that the only true Parent is God—that same

Creating God whom they have, consciously or unconsciously, supplanted as Father-Mother the moment they became parents themselves.

For the awakened Being, the departure of either a loved one or anyone else is a celebration; for the human being asleep to his own Being and Parents, death is a tragedy.

Once we accept the process of death in Life, everything is much more cheerful, bearable, and simple. The impotence and frustration transform themselves naturally into Peace and acceptance. Resentment and fear become joy and excitement.

Mourning the death of a loved one with a mixture of nostalgia for someone who we will never again see with this body is completely understandable and legitimate, as long as it is done consciously and with joy. Even if you don't understand it, the Being of that person has decided to continue its path free of its "burdensome material body," and if we desire it, you will meet again to share fresh universal adventures on the paths of the so-called "eternity."

Sadness as a Disconnection From Yourself

If we look at statistics pertaining to sadness that leads to depression, we see that it increases in proportion to age. Depression is more common in adolescents than it is in children, is more prevalent in young people than in adolescents, and much more common in adults than in young people, and highest in the elderly compared to adults.

What do you think is the cause?

The more we age, the more time we spend disconnected from ourselves, from our Being, from our own Knowledge. As the time nears for us to abandon this body, we internally know—whether we admit it or not—that we have not done what we came here to do, that we haven't kept our promises. Nor have we expanded the Love of God Father-Mother or been the example of tenderness, richness, and Happiness that we set out to be for our earthly parents, Mom and Dad.

Time passes, and as the probability of leaving this body increases, people get scared. They are frightened by what lies ahead.

I think of Pilar, a Catholic woman of fervent religious beliefs. She had been a nun for a good portion of her life. The day she came to have sessions with me, at ninety-two years of age, she was stricken with profound depression. Pilar was ashamed to confess that she was terrified by the idea of dying. Although her mind told her that she had led the life of a good Christian woman, according to human law, and that God was waiting to welcome her, inwardly she had the sensation that there was something that she had not done right. She didn't know what (or so she said at first), but she felt guilty for it, and she was sure about it.

Recognizing that she had turned her back on the God Father-Mother, alive in herself, and had elected to maintain cold judgments about others and simple human beliefs, she vehemently said, "I can't forgive myself for this!"

I still remember her face upon finishing our first session. She looked like a five-year-old girl, free, happy, and thrilled that she had just rediscovered the most important thing for a child: she had once more found her Parents, and they hadn't turned their backs on her at any time, nor were they judging her. Three hours were enough to restore the smile of that woman, generous and humble deep down inside. Three hours in which she re-established contact with her Being, with her Creator, and with the Father-Mother for Eternity.

Two more years would pass before Pilar left her body to continue on her path in peace and without any fear, two years during which we shared a lovely friendship. She asked me to sit beside her on her deathbed and there, in a gesture of infinite tenderness, she kissed my hand and gave me a wonderful letter she had written to me and which I have kept to this day.

Dearest Anne,

There are no words to express how grateful I am that God placed you in my path. The day I met you I began to live and breathe Love, on that day I awakened from an immense slumber from which, without your tender, patient, and loving help, I would not have been able to escape.

For the first time in my life, although this is often said, I feel content with the years I've lived on our wonderful Earth, and feel at peace with myself.

The hour awaits me, and I face it completely at ease and with great hope. I feel a tickle in my stomach. It's an emotion that I've never felt before, and it makes me smile. Ha, ha, I think I'm in love. Yes, dear, I'm in love with God.

Wait, now I remember a day that I felt something similar to this. It was the day my father first took me to see the sea. Oh, Anne, what emotion! I know it because I feel it, that our Parents, and maybe even my mom and dad, are waiting for me with their arms wide open.

It can't be any other way because, as you know, after having regretted and forgiven myself completely, I have absolutely no doubt that they love us, like you well say: Our Parents.

I will always keep the memory of you in, as you call them, my loveliest and most luminous atoms. I will cherish the memory of your luminous gaze as I embark on my new path.

I love you my precious little angel. Run along and awaken them all.

I await in Glory,
María del Pilar

Act Now

If sadness is the opposite of action, what better remedy is there than to get moving in order to alleviate this sadness?

If you feel sad, think about which circumstances or situations of your life are causing you to feel this way. Think about what it is that makes you feel powerless, what it is that you wish were different and that makes you think that there is no way out.

Once you've realized what it is, don't waste another second complaining about your bad luck. Get moving, and do something to change your situation. Ask for help, do whatever it takes, but transform the impotence and inactivity that belong to darkness into decisions and solutions that wait for you in your Heart. Your knowledge is waiting for you there, intact.

Alison was a middle-aged housewife in a small town in Virginia. Her life revolved around her husband and her two sons who had already left home, Chris and Earl. Alison had come to me feeling sad, powerless, frustrated, and angry at her younger son Chris's decision to move to Canada with his girlfriend.

It didn't take long for Alison to laugh at the absurdity of her own anger, when she realized that her son was actually demonstrating great courage in venturing out to discover the world and seek his own Happiness. This was a yearning she had long felt herself but had never dared to fulfill. Alison understood that, until that moment, bored with her own life, she had tried to live it vicariously through her children and others, such as family members and neighbors. It was no longer enough to fill her day-to-day life or to give her that joy that she so intensely longed for.

Searching for the natural talents that could help her become involved, we found cooking, but more specifically, baking incredible cakes. In fact, she was known in her village for being a good cook and only using natural products, Her fruit pies, with fruit from her own garden, were especially renowned. It didn't take many sessions with me for Alison to decide to make use of her passion and begin to sell her pies to her neighbors. Before long, a health food store began commissioning dozens of cakes from her a day.

Alison finally felt alive, joyful, and active as never before. She had rediscovered her joy, the joy that she had so fearfully lost due to the estrangement of her children. She thanked me repeatedly for having accompanied her and awakened her to the Reality in which our Parents love her and are waiting for her.

Her company grew rapidly, and today she has the means and the time to visit her son and to travel as often as the whim takes her—and believe me, it takes her plenty.

Part Four

To Evolve Is Your
Sole Responsibility

Being Happy Is an Altruistic Act

Being happy is not only not a selfish act but, in fact,
is your only duty on Earth.

In the collective unconscious, there is a widespread message that teaches us that being happy is selfish, that it is something bad. Simply put, being happy is frowned upon. How many times have I heard my students say things like: "How can I be happy with all the suffering there is in the world?" or "Being happy is a selfish act," "Through my suffering, I will get to heaven," "Being happy is not right," "Being happy is utopian," "I can only allow myself to be happy for a few moments, then I start to think about things and lapse into sadness again."

Unhappiness as Punishment

In general, human beings prefer to remain in what they believe is the deserved punishment dictated by the voice of their ego, which helps them atone for the intrinsic guilt they feel. Incapable of freeing themselves from this feeling of guilt they drag around, most people punish themselves, thereby giving themselves the impression that they are paying for all the errors of the past, including those of others, in this life and in past lives.

Society, albeit unconsciously, teaches us that it is bad to be happy while others are suffering. It also instills in us the notion that suffering in this life is the only way to atone for our transgressions and ensure a better experience when it comes time to abandon our body and pass on to another plane. This belief, however, flies in the face of all the laws of physics, of Reality, and of the genuine loving Essence of our Creating Parents.

Social Recognition

Society has always more readily commended and applauded those who feel bad or suffer as opposed to those who feel good and enjoy themselves. It is true that the simple fact of feeling distressed or morose can garner recognition from your social group or society as a whole, but actually, is this helping to improve your predicament, or is it fueling and intensifying it?

Choose What to Focus On

What sense does it make for you to also feel bad because others on this planet are suffering or because there is darkness on this planet to begin with?

Let's return for a moment to the metaphor of the blackboard, which is predominantly dark and on which you have the power to draw, using the chalk of your choice. Facing this blackboard, which symbolizes darkness, what would happen if you chose to draw on it with black chalk? Naturally, the blackboard would not gain in beauty or in luminosity. The dark chalk of your suffering would only serve to add more darkness and pain to that which is already there. The darkness would remain dark. Will you have helped to diminish suffering in this way?

No, of course not. Your suffering, your sadness, your pain, whatever its nature, will never have a positive impact on the suffering of others or your own.

Imagine that you have a friend who tells you he is devastated because his wife confessed to having a lover and has left him. Between sobs, he tells you that he fears that he will never find or love another woman, and what is worse, that he will no longer be able to trust anyone.

Would you begin to cry with him and tell him that indeed life is awful and that you cannot trust anybody? Sounds absurd, doesn't it? Then what sense does it make for the human being to do exactly this in the face of the suffering of others?

This does not mean that when we hear or see or feel the pain or suffering of others we should not feel anything or remain indifferent.

Far from it. Any given human being in their Heart sometimes feels sadness when confronted with the suffering of others. Nonetheless, he can immediately choose to rid his space of this sadness. We can all feel—in agreement with our Hearts—compassion, courage, and determination. Suffering and Ignorance in this world remind me of my decision and my mission at every juncture: to awaken others to their own Heart.

You must realize that it is not a question of being indifferent to what is going on around you in the world. Obviously not. But if you're looking to help diminish the world's suffering, as many people already are, the first thing you can and must do is increase your own loving thoughts and acts in your daily life, liberate your Love throughout your personal expression. As paradoxical as it may seem to your ego-manipulated mind, the only thing that you can do to have a positive impact in the lives of the suffering is to enjoy yourself as much as possible and share this Happiness, thereby increasing your affection and love on this planet that you currently inhabit.

A while ago, I remember reading how Mother Teresa of Calcutta used to say to the nuns in her order that if they didn't feel happy they shouldn't bother getting up in the morning. For her, feeling happy was first and foremost a duty, a prerequisite for being able to help others. Happiness is a state and an expression of Love, and just like God, it is unconditional.

REMEMBER: When we focus our attention on something, in reality we are intensifying it and co-creating it with our minds. When we feel pain or sadness, we are connecting ourselves to the vibrational currents of those who are suffering, thereby fueling and causing them to grow.

Let's Elevate the Vibrational Level of the Planet

Imagine that the moment everyone has so affectionately been waiting for has arrived—the moment when millions of people the world over choose, voluntarily, to focus on their Heart and allow themselves to be joyful. As a result, the vibrational level of the planet is elevated. The circulating energy currents are now predominantly loving and luminous, so the probability of other people plugging into them is considerably higher.

The practical results? Having less people connected to dark currents means suffering would diminish exponentially: less abuse, less mistreatment, less distress, less illness, less pain, less torture, less war, less tyranny, less horror, more Love, more complicity, more Happiness, more respect, more art, more Beauty, and so on.

You too can do your bit by using your Heart, your loving intelligence, your richness and business sense, your joy and your compassion, your science, etc.

Helping Requires Inner Maturity

To be happy is your only duty on Earth. Happiness is the emotional manifestation of your inner Peace and the creating force of your permanent Well-Being. Feeling happy is the most natural and simple way you have to co-create and share with your fellows. Can you imagine a more altruistic act than enhancing the Love of this dark universe?

You might be asking yourself: And what happens to all of those disadvantaged people who are in need of help? If from deep within the Knowledge of your Being, you feel that it is part of your personal mission to give something more back, to dedicate your life, or part of it, to bettering the lives of the disadvantaged, that's fine, but don't become impatient, as when it's time to follow through on this deeply felt conviction, your Being will let you know.

Remember that although there are countries and populations subject to extreme poverty and need, many times we forget that the first person we need to help, to be able to help others in turn, is ourselves. First of all, make sure that you have reclaimed your Power, that you have subdued your ego, and healed your emotional system, then and only then will you be able to help those who wish to be helped, from the Light of your Heart.

Imagine a young boy trying to carry his disabled and sick grandmother before having grown up himself. Give yourself time to grow.

Helping is Not Assisting

On this planet, fraught with confusion, we many times mistake helping with assisting. It's not rare for people to assist those who are disadvantaged, instead of helping them find their own way out of the needy situation in which they find themselves.

The human being asleep to his Reality seeks anything to have a clear conscience.

Furthermore, remember that in this universe in which we live, nothing is random. The fact that a Being chooses to live in certain situations is not arbitrary. Only the Being itself can fathom the reasons it chooses to live through a particular experience, as harsh, unjust, and painful as it may seem in the eyes of others.

This is why it is vital that we offer help and do not impose it. We must allow people to choose whether they wish to find a way out of their situation or not, and at what pace and how they wish to do so. Let's offer and show them the tools they already have that will permit them not only to escape their predicament but never to find themselves in a similar situation again.

If you notice, you can clearly see that it isn't necessary to travel thousands of miles to find someone who wants and seeks your help. Remain in your own Well-being and internal peace, and you'll see how he who truly needs your help and wants to make a change will come looking for you because he sees that he can trust you. Furthermore, by acting from your Heart on a daily basis you will already be helping, without consciously meaning to do it, all those people with whom you interact.

As an anecdote, I can tell you that the moment you begin to spend more time in your Heart than in your ego, you will even notice animals seeking you out and babies looking at you and smiling. They can easily see that willing Heart and that joyous presence without you having to do or say anything special.

This Dark Universe Wants You to Love It and Offer It Your Joy

Have you ever stopped to think about the sheer quantity of Beings that come and go on this planet constantly? According to statistics, every day there are approximately 360,000 Beings incarnated on this planet and 155,000 Beings that leave their bodies.

What do you think is the reason behind this continuous wave of Beings that come and go on this planet? What reasons could underlie this rationally inexplicable and imperceptible daily reality? I can only give you the answer from the Knowledge that resides in you as much as it does in me: to increase Love and its Light. The darkness that surrounds us and is part of us seeks to be transformed, loved, and filled with joy and eternal life. This universe in which we live wishes us to love it and give it Life.

According to the principle of Evolution, everything, absolutely everything that exists in this universe, looks to be awakened to Love and its infinite expressions.

It is vitally important that you awaken and reclaim your Happiness. The reasons for this are manifold:

- Your Being evolves (returns Home) by listening to its loving Knowledge, and in this way, is able to fulfill its promises in your day-to-day life. If your person allows your Being to do its work, It will increase its luminous capital, which will allow It to travel to more light-filled places and find its way back Home to God Father-Mother.
- Being happier when you abandon your body than when you entered it.
- Your current life on this planet is transformed into a more pleasant experience of joy, well-being, and abundance.
- You serve as an example to others so that they may also focus on their Hearts.
- You serve as an example to your biological parents.
- You help to alleviate the Dark chain that links you to your ancestors.

- You are contributing to increasing the Health and Well-Being of the planet and of the universe itself.

Fulfill the promises you made before you were born. Walk along your entire path with a Heart that is willing to Love, wherever you may go or whatever you may do.

Perhaps now you are asking yourself: What can I do to awaken myself to my Happiness on this planet?

As we will explore in the following chapters, in order to feel happy, you will need to recognize Yourself, evolve by sharing your Heart and Knowledge in your relations with others, engage in a profession that inspires you and yields great benefits, recover the teachings of your Being, offer your body the care it needs, and take care of the planet just as you promised you would.

Will you come along with me?

CHAPTER 25

Relationships as the Motor of Evolution

In each moment of our lives, we have the option of aligning ourselves with the growing Light of our awakened Heart or with the relentless and dark voice of our ego. You can choose!

Human relationships provide us with the perfect scenario for our evolution. If your sole duty as a human being consists in expressing Love in your daily experience, and for it to occur you need to feel emotions of different vibrational levels, then human relationships are the arena in which you will be able to experience them.

As Beings, we must realize that if we didn't need to interact with others to be able to evolve, we wouldn't inhabit a planet with over seven billion people. Instead, we would simply be alone. But that isn't the case, is it? We are made to interact with other Beings, and to grow in the process.

It is in our relations with others that we will be in a position to experience the entire spectrum of possible emotions. It is precisely these emotions that will allow us to evolve. In cases in which the emotion is negative, this gives you the opportunity to grow, bring light to the negative emotion, and subdue your ego in the process.

REMEMBER: Whenever the emotion you feel is loving, you will be automatically increasing your Light.

Who do you think has more chances of feeling emotions and evolving—you or a person who lives isolated in a house without contact with the outside world?

Granted, no matter how much a person tries to isolate himself, she will still feel emotions, but the range of these emotions will be considerably impoverished.

Look at the variety of possible interactions that this life has to offer us. In a single day and in a single place, you can meet Beings who have just arrived and others who are on the verge of departing; you can meet the rich, the poor, the healthy, the ill, the fanatical, the open and tolerant, beggars, successful entrepreneurs, children, adults, celebrities...

Align Yourself with Your Heart, and Express Your Light in Harmony with Your Interactions

Life offers us different levels of well-being or distress, with the sole aim of having us take a position when we face them. Human relationships, every meeting with another human, helps us to identify ourselves with our Heart or with our ego, thus aligning ourselves with one or the other.

Naturally, you don't feel the same walking through a luxurious and very pleasant neighborhood as you do walking through a poor one, or walking through one inhabited principally by entrepreneurs and executives as opposed to working-class people.

The emotional reactions and sensations are different. But what is the real aim of this wide range of options?

By having daily contact with these different classes and realities that co-exist in our world, something in us makes us position ourselves immediately and clearly. There will be things with which you can identify yourself and others that you cannot. There will be people who feel more at ease in a modest neighborhood than in an affluent or luxurious one and others that will need a middle-class neighborhood to feel at home. Aligning ourselves in favor of our evolution implies that we choose at every moment. Each instant of life requires a choice by you. That is what we clearly are: choices.

Your Relationship to Money

It's clear to most people that wealth does not necessarily equal Happiness. Although material abundance is very important on a planet that is itself material, this doesn't mean that an affluent neighborhood is happier than a humbler one, or that a person with a big bank account is automatically a better person while a person in debt is not.

But this isn't automatically true; quite the opposite. There are many people in upper socio-economic levels who are just as loving as others. People who allow themselves to enjoy abundance and comfort in their lives have understood, unlike many others, that on this material planet we have come to enjoy material comfort, too.

Nature herself shows this to us. She tirelessly shares her bounty with all of her children in order to nurture our well-being. It's not her fault that some of her children have problems with math and do not know how to distribute her wealth equitably, even as others complain but let it happen.

On a material planet, money is instrumental in the achievement of a certain level of comfort, and therefore for manifesting well-being and greater Happiness. As Beings, we were born on this planet to experience pleasure and enjoyment through the organizational Intelligence of the Heart.

What would you enjoy more: a small dark studio or a lovely and luminous house in the country surrounded by nature and fresh air? Would you prefer to drive a small, outdated car that consumes a lot of gas and contaminates more, or a new and comfortable car with low CO_2 emissions that can protect you and your family from potential dangers on the highway? Would you prefer to eat all the healthy, natural, and tasty foods that maintain your health, even when only specialized stores carry them, or do you prefer to consume unhealthful conventional, modern products full of saturated fats, pesticides, wheat, transgenic products, and white sugar?

Align Yourself With Your Heart

Let's continue exploring the possibilities that our relations with others can provide us for our evolution.

Picture yourself walking down a street. What emotions would you experience when meeting one of the following: an ill child in a wheelchair, a healthy adolescent, a poor elderly woman alone and disoriented, a transvestite, a soldier in uniform, a beggar, a thief, an attractive businesswoman, a young disabled person, a nun, a drug addict, an adolescent dressed to provoke, a woman pushing a baby carriage, a man with a sad and forlorn look in his eyes, or a group of friends laughing?

The emotional reactions that you, like anybody else, will have when faced with this spectrum of people will undoubtedly be varied. Just as your emotional reaction to all of these situations and people will be utterly different from what mine or that of other people may be.

Let's take the example of the sick child in a wheelchair. *Et voilá*, imagine the possibility has presented itself.

If you choose, you can listen to the voice of your ego and feel pity or indifference for the boy, spending long moments thinking about how unfortunate he is and how much his parents must be suffering, how horrible it would be if this were to happen to someone close to you, dwelling endlessly on these thoughts and your distress, as well as the sadness and powerlessness that they provoke in you. Or you choose not to think about him even for a moment.

But you can also choose, from the greatness of your own Heart, to see that this body you perceive as a boy, is in fact a Being that is thousands of years old; that the reasons his Being has chosen this experience is none of your business. Instead, you offer him a smile or an authentic look filled with Love, to show that unconditional Love is everyone's business.

You can align yourself in each moment. The choice is always and only yours.

Your Friends Are Your Family of the Heart

Become aware for a moment of the endless wave of Beings that are coming and going on our beloved planet Earth, right now, at the very moment you are reading this sentence. All of us, as Beings who inhabit this universe, are interconnected, united by an immense network of vibrational, and more or less, luminous connections.

Human beings are social by nature. They are made to share, to love and be loved, to give and receive, to feel useful and to allow others to feel the same. Not to fully explore the possibilities of all these interactions would make no sense at all.

The friends with whom you choose to share your years on Earth are what I would call your family of the Heart. Your biological parents and siblings are the family of origin that your Being selected to remind you what not to do and learn to share your love or to forgive. Friends, once aligned with your level of maturity, are the family you chose to lovingly accompany, and to be lovingly accompanied by, on your path on this planet.

Few people succeed in enjoying genuine friendships, relationships based on Love, in which you can share pleasures as well as overcome obstacles in life—friends who, because they Love, forgive, and respect themselves, are capable of being the same way with you. This friendship is very different from one where one "friend" needs to seduce, manipulate, and even buy friends, whom he later criticizes whenever he gets a chance.

The Couple as a Motor of Your Evolution

After your relationship with your biological parents, the relationship with your partner is the one that will offer you the perfect environment to experience your most profound, intense, and in most cases, painful emotions.

For the ego, it is an enticing playground where it can bring its entire dark arsenal, putting you to the test in front of your needs, pains and traumas experienced in your childhood and youth. The relationship with a loved one offers the perfect scenario to relive all the painful and negative emotions of our childhood.

A relationship of genuine Love, that is, a relationship born of two Beings that meet and share their Love, independently of the bodies they have chosen to use for this earthly experience, is a rare occurrence on this planet.

On Earth, in general, people who come together to form a couple and lead a life together are attracted to physical aspects of each other rather than aspects of their respective Beings. This is the reason there are so many emotional hardships, so many broken relationships, and so many hurt and vulnerable people. We are brought together by fickle, fleeting, and ephemeral attributes that sooner or later will lead to the end of the relationship.

Although infrequent, the relationship between two Beings that meet, recognize each other, and continue their eternal evolutionary journey together through this and other worlds is also possible here on Earth. When this happens, it is the most precious gift that we can accept to receive in our Lives: sharing our Love, our Life (our eternity) with another Being that, like us, chooses to continue evolving.

In general, relationships between couples are not a topic I address in my individual sessions. The task of awakening oneself to one's own Happiness is a very personal challenge; only when this is accomplished can a person meet another person and Love in the biggest sense of the word. Can we love another person if we can't first love ourselves first, if we carry around guilt, fear, sadness, rancor, and self-punishment?

If you haven't accepted responsibility for your own Happiness, you will end up expecting your partner to make you feel happy, eventually leading you to disappointment, frustration, and powerlessness when you realize that your partner had the same expectations about you.

The role of the couple in society is a very delicate topic, one that is susceptible to misunderstandings and unpleasantness. It is not uncommon to find people or societies that are opposed to one or another form of relationship between couples: same-sex couples, couples with considerable age differences or economic situations, interracial couples, couples from different religious backgrounds, and so forth. If we think about it, why should it matter to us what others do or do not do with their lives or with their bodies?

As Beings, we have come to continue evolving, loving, and not judging anybody for their choices. If our mission in this life had been to evolve in the place of others, we would doubtlessly have been granted the power to think through their minds, feel through their Hearts, and see through their eyes, or choose for others through their I, but that's not the case.

Everyone has enough with their own inner work without trying to change everyone else at all costs. Every time we try to force changes on the behavior of others, we are neglecting ourselves. You can't be in two places at once, and there is a reason for that.

The majority of these preconceptions and judgments about how things should or shouldn't be done are learned from others. You've copied them. They are not yours. They certainly do not belong to your Heart, but rather to your darkness—the darkest part, in fact.

God, Father-Mother, our Creating Essence, only wants you to manifest your Love and to spread Light. Who spreads more Love—two people who love one another or one who judges and criticizes them? What does the Essence expect of you? Love and benevolence or criticism and judgment?

Every time you focus your attention or dwell on something that you don't like or don't think is right, you are turning your back on your Power and blindly following the dark paths of judgment marked by your unruly and tyrannical ego.

The moment you criticize or accuse another, you are plugging yourself into a dark current that will only serve to bring more of the same into your own life. Without a doubt, if you prioritize judgment and criticism at the expense of compassion and acceptance, sooner or later *you* will be the one to be judged by others; *you* will be the victim of an injustice or ostracized, and *you* will find it just as unfair. What goes around comes around.

After all, who benefits from you trying to run the lives of others? It annoys the people on the receiving end, makes you feel worse, and serves as an example to those around you, who will likely imitate it, so what good *does* it do?

REMEMBER: In your chest beats a Heart! Look inside your Heart, and you'll see that only compassion and empathy live there. As expressions of Love they will become your daily allies in any relationship you begin.

CHAPTER 26

Your Job at the Service
of Your Happiness

As we know, the Being that decides to be incarnated in a human body does so with the clear purpose of continuing to evolve through its earthly experience. But can we really be mindful of our Being and our Heart if we spend long hours immersed in mental work in the workplace? How can we evolve if we neglect our Power in the face of our ever-demanding mind?

Human beings are designed to spend a large part of their days in service to their Beings, listening to the voice of its Knowledge, creating their experiences, and enjoying their own paths. But the reality, at least for the majority of people, is very different. Between work and the rest of the obligations of the average adult, there is little time, if any, left over to spend with himself, in the peace and creativity of his inner self.

The paradox is that, in many cases, of all the hours that people spend at work, only a small fraction of them are truly productive, necessary, and effective.

According to recent statistics, 80 percent of North Americans are dissatisfied with their job.

The good news is that there is an alternative. People who are centered in their Heart and aware of the Knowledge that resides in their Being clearly see what they have to do, see or realize in every moment of the day. Because of this, they are much more effective and efficient and can shorten their otherwise interminable working day.

Granted, this might seem utopian to some, but tell me, what would happen if companies dedicated a part of their day to allowing their employees to be free, in touch with their inner selves, or at least encouraged to take such moments? Before long they would see benefits to the company, as the efficiency and satisfaction would increase while the working day would be shortened by several hours. Absenteeism would be minimized, and loyalty to the company would rise exponentially.

The Three Aims of Work

As Beings, we come to this planet with the purpose of dedicating a limited portion of our day to work. This work should have three aims: to co-create through the innate Knowledge in our Heart, to contribute something to society, and to earn lots of money doing it.

Co-Creating Through the Peace and Richness of Your Heart

The Being comes into the world with the aim of manifesting its creativity through the work that it does once incarnated. It comes to co-create daily through its Light.

The work performed by the person incarnated by this Being should simply be an extension of its evolutionary task, another way to follow its path back Home. How will it evolve more? By creating through Happiness and well-being or working through a mind tricked by the ego and ignorant of its inner passenger?

An architect who creates a beautiful home or building from his passion and joy will evolve. But will the architect who designs a military building or a nuclear plant do so?

REMEMBER: We human beings have the innate power to create our own experience in this and in other worlds. So how would you like to shape the reality that you are creating and recreating?

Contribute Something to Society

Try to imagine for a moment a society built from the Loving Essence and its efficient mind, and not from a mind absorbed and focused on its ignorant human ego.

Yes, every one of us has something good to contribute to the society in which we live, and it would be legitimate to receive, in exchange, everything needed to live a comfortable and happy life. We would dedicate a few hours of our precious time to the necessary work to make sure things function smoothly, and the rest of the time would be dedicated to enjoying an art or to enjoying the company of loved ones or one's own company and inner life.

People would not have to survive, or struggle to do so. They would not have to spend most of their lives working with the sole purpose of paying their mortgage or their car payments or the school fees of their children or the countless monthly bills. Nobody would have to live with the fear of losing their job or their health insurance, because each one of us would have our assigned task, which we would perform with determination. It would be a society in which each one of us would contribute something, and we would all receive something from others. People would feel happy and at peace. We would dedicate our lives to enjoyment, spreading our unconditional Love in this universe, and by doing so, we would feel in harmony with the Promise made to our Creating Parents.

Utopia? It is our only duty.

Can you imagine an entire society working like this?

Of course, I know that things are very different now, and that the way in which the world is made is not easily reconcilable with this reality of the Being. But we always have the individual choice of living this reality by choosing a profession that allows us to use our Heart and our innate creativity and contribute something to society.

Earn a Lot of Money Doing It

From childhood, through our first interactions with the adults around us, we got the message that earning money is difficult, or that we must work hard and for long hours to be able to earn enough of it to enjoy the things that are in fact very basic: a house, a safe car, healthy food, health insurance, clothing, education, and so on.

Most people carry these messages with them, at least unconsciously, throughout their lives. But where do you think these messages come from: the Heart or the worried and submissive ego?

We are here to convert this human experience into a pleasurable experience, one of well-being, enjoyment, and delight. Given the way our society is conceived, to do that it is necessary to earn considerable amounts of money.

Now that you have the three aims of work in mind, you can clearly see that for the vast majority of human beings, the reality of work is actually very different.

Money: Your Power to Act

Ask anyone living in a highly consumerist society if they would like to have lots of money, and with a few rare exceptions they will say yes. But, as in the case of Happiness, although they all want it, few think they deserve it, and few allow themselves to enjoy it.

It is common for people to think that having lots of money is not for them, that it is reserved for the few who are graced by fortune, or that it is something bad or selfish, or that they will only be able to enjoy financial security and comfort after many years of hard work and effort and personal sacrifice.

Things are very different when people understand from the outset that this material world is more than willing to offer us all the abundance of material goods that we could possibly wish to enjoy. Planet Earth is a material planet, with material things, objects, and money.

On a few occasions, when we touch on the subject of money, a student of mine will speak of his firm belief that money is not important for Happiness. True, we are already happy by nature, but to help this Happiness materialize on a daily basis, money is also one of our greatest allies.

This is a material planet and because of it we have to play by its rules.

You will undoubtedly have heard phrases like "money can't buy Happiness," and of course, nothing can buy the state of Happiness. But to be happy in this material world we need a host of material possessions, and these material possessions are generally acquired with money.

Having coffee with friends or inviting them over to your house for a meal requires money. You will also need a lot of money to feed your family healthy natural foods. Just 50 years ago, buying junk food was the exception; now, what's natural has become scarce and extremely expensive and beyond the everyday budget. It's all a question of money. Even drinking water that's not bad for your health isn't affordable for everybody.

What has happened with the most basic and essential elements for the life and health of the body? If the planet hasn't poisoned its elements, who has? Not the animals, not the plants, not the weather. Only human beings have this level of intelligence and internal immaturity.

When I speak of material well-being and financial plenty, I'm not referring to owning an enormous and luxurious mansion, although if that makes you happy, then why not? The important thing is that you have enough money to enjoy living in a house that is ideal for you, to eat healthy and natural foods, to give your children, if you have them, a good education, to drive a safe and nice car, to be able to travel to exotic places when you wish to; in short, to be able to enjoy all the good that this Life has to offer on this planet of abundance, but now contaminated by its most intelligent children.

So, if money is an ally of our Happiness and a necessary and desirable companion, why is it that most people don't have all the money they desire and need?

Simply because they haven't understood the rules of the game. They have not understood that money is really our friend and ally.

Conditioned by the negative messages they have recorded in their minds regarding money, people end up viewing it as something to fear. In a sense, they banish it from their lives. To the extent that they are willing to accept this state of affairs, the energy current of money and abundance simply strays and doesn't reach them.

In my courses, I often use the following metaphor, which has proved useful for those who work with it.

Picture money as a friend. Imagine that every time this loyal friend comes to see you, you share your problems with him. You talk about your shortcomings and your frustrations, you complain, then at the end of the visit, you blame your friend for all of your unhappiness, because he doesn't come to see you often enough. The next time this friend thinks about visiting you, he will likely think twice and decide to visit a more affable person, someone who would be happy to see him, a more grateful person who enjoys being with him, who seeks him out for who and what he really is.

In order to make peace with this great friend, Mr. Money, you need to make peace with yourself and reeducate and reassure your ego first.

CHAPTER 27

Education for Happiness

The conventional education of children serves to prepare them for the competitive labor market and the working masses. It invades and manipulates their minds, molding them into new armies of marionettes for society and the labor market. It is an education that, in general, favors thought over sentiment, knowledge over Knowledge, the selfish mind over the intelligence of the Heart, and memorization over creativity.

Where do you think the roots of this type of education lie: in the Heart or in the ego?

How many things do you remember from all those years you spent studying in school? Maybe a tenth, or perhaps, if you've got a good memory, a quarter. Don't you think that all that knowledge we acquired over the years spent sitting and domesticated could have been learned in a quarter of the time?

The biological parents of these kids, themselves obliged by the system to work long hours, need to leave their kids in an institution that will educate them and where they can spend time with other kids. And here we come upon the other great excuse to keep kids in classrooms for endless hours: socialization. We've all heard that children need to socialize in order to mature and develop in an appropriate manner. However, if you look closely, you'll see that it's in classrooms that socializing is least encouraged. It is precisely in classrooms where children learn to feel alone in the crowd.

As surrounded as the child may be by classmates while facing the teacher in front, lecturing the class, she is alone.

We all inwardly sense that there is something more that exists, that the Knowledge in our Heart expects our attention. Going to school and seeing that nobody talks about this, each child feels alone among her classmates, estranged without realizing that everyone else feels the same way. It's then when the child truly feels abandoned on this planet. This illustrates the total lack of communication that exists between kids at school. If instead they were to talk about it honestly, not like marionettes imitating others, they would remember this; they would realize that they are not alone in their desolation.

Children learn early on to give priority to the mind, to forget their emotions and the genuine physical needs of their bodies. The human body is made principally to be in motion. And yet, young people spend long hours sitting in the same position in the often uncomfortable chairs offered by conventional schools.

It is indeed true that society needs a profound change in direction to return to the Essence of what it came here to embody. But in the meantime, we can at least initiate changes that can teach future adults new ways of living, without adversely affecting them in their own Essence.

Education for Happiness

What would be the results of an education for children based on the values of the Being that inhabits them instead of those of the ego-mind? Are all the subjects in current curricula actually necessary for children? How many of the things we learn in those long years of study will prove of benefit to us in our everyday lives? How many of the things we learn will help us to be happy and to succeed?

How many square roots do you use in your daily life? Personally, I've never used a single square root in my life. Unless you need it for your job, what is the use of being forced to learn something that has no other purpose than to domesticate the mind and favor it over the emotions? In how many situations has it been useful to know by memory the list of kings that reigned in the Europe of the past?

I'm not saying that general culture is not useful or necessary; on the contrary, it is important to know the world in which we live because of the choices and experiences of our ancestors. I am saying, however, that there are other forms of transmitting this information, without resorting to an abstract and insipid memorization of lengthy texts.

How different academic results would be if instead of being forced to sit and fix their attention on classroom lectures and later on their books at home, we encouraged students to use their bodies and emotions, their sensitivity in learning. For instance, if we presented history for what it is: an interesting vision of those who tell it, one that allows us to better understand the past.

What if, instead of spending years sitting in frigid classrooms studying and learning, we had been given the same information by our teachers but while walking in nature, or while making bread with our hands or sitting under a tree, or visiting a businessman, so that he could tell us how he achieved success and how the reality of economics works on this planet? Wouldn't that have been far more interesting to us?

The beauty and intensity of those moments of conviviality would have helped you understand everything the teacher was conveying to you and make it your own. And all that without having to suffer the highly contentious examinations that we are subject to in the traditional education system, which aims to classify us with a number indicating what we're going to become or not become in order to have professional success and be upstanding workers.

Not only would the intellectual results have been far superior but the opportunities for initiating relationships with other students and the teacher would have been much greater as well. There might then have been space to accommodate our individuality and identity, and a closeness to our teacher that would have permitted us to express our concerns on any given subject, thereby learning about life while also learning about human relations—not least emotions, which are so often forgotten and form the basis of all our experience.

The Curriculum of Education
for Happiness and Success

The aim of educating our children and having them go to school is to enable them to be happy and enjoy life as adults. If parents want them to study and do so at the best schools, it's so that one day they will have the chance to succeed in their profession and earn a good living.

If you were to ask people with kids what they wish for them, many, if not all, would mention at least one of three things: that they be happy, healthy, and financially successful.

If the purpose of education is to create happy, successful, and healthy adults, what do you think a school curriculum should look like? It might be something like this:

SUBJECT 1: Teach them to recognize themselves as eternal Beings in an ephemeral human body, as Children of God Father-Mother. Help them to privilege a space in their day for establishing a personal communication with the Creator of their own lives, discover and get to know the planet upon which they have recently arrived, without forgetting the universe that

186

they inhabit. All this by teaching them the importance of respecting the Reality in which they live and how to handle themselves in the society to which they belong during this earthly life.

SUBJECT 2: Remind them of the importance of their own innate individuality. In a society that prizes the external over the internal, it is vital to encourage kids to pay attention to their inner selves, to be in permanent connection with their Heart, and to always use their own computer, the mind, in personally beneficial ways.

This subject takes on even more importance in an era in which we have replaced the enjoyment of playing in the streets with friends with playing on computers or cell phones, and substituted the Knowledge that resides within us with the answers and false challenges we find on a web browser.

SUBJECT 3: Teach them to discover the power of their Hearts and their emotions to create experiences. Teach them how to deal with these experiences and release the undesirable ones. Teach them to know their ego, to deal with educating it, and to reassure it until its voice stops being an obstacle to their day-to-day existence. Teach them to cry from a place of courage when they wish to free themselves from pain, to forgive themselves and make new decisions, instead of complaining like a victim who wallows in pain.

SUBJECT 4: Teach them to know the body they inhabit, to understand its warnings to take care of it, and to heal it if necessary. Teach them the foods and plants that are beneficial to their health and when and how to use them. Teach them to grow and cook their own food in the most appetizing and healthy manner.

SUBJECT 5: Teach them what we know of the principles that govern this universe so that they can understand the rules of the game of life. In this way, they can create their own favorable experiences from the intelligence of their Hearts, with the help of the multiple aptitudes and talents they already have with them after being born on this planet.

SUBJECT 6: Teach them what money is, that it is important, and that they should see it as a friend. Show them how to earn and enjoy money and let it flow freely in their lives.

SUBJECT 7: Teach them how the society we live in works, its rules, its structure, and markets. All children should understand the aspects relevant to their practical lives, and ideally, once they have decided on what they would like to do, they should be provided with a mentor to educate them further.

SUBJECT 8: Teach them general culture and applied knowledge (mathematics, geography, science, and so forth) through the use of experiments and attentive listening, without memorizing and without having them sit motionless in a classroom. Within the teachings of general culture, it is fundamental that they be told the history of humanity and in particular how the human being has behaved over the centuries, how it has principally encouraged darkness, poisoning the planet and "occupying" the mind of the world's population so that nobody realizes. So, that they can clearly see the consequences of those selfish acts.

SUBJECT 9: Teach them one or more types of artistic activities: playing a musical instrument, painting, singing, dancing, modeling, and so on. Art allows one to co-create Beauty amplifying the Light in oneself, in one's surroundings, on this planet, and in the universe at large.

Can you imagine the impact of starting to apply this kind of curriculum to the lives and education of our children? Apart from having a full and happy childhood, they will become happy adults. From Peace, they will create Joy, achieve success in their lives, meet their partner through Love not fear, take care of the planet and its natural legacy, serve as examples of Happiness for other generations, and undoubtedly attain whatever their Heart can desire.

CHAPTER 28

You Promised Yourself to Take Care of Your Vehicle

Illness and distress are nothing more than the
warnings of our Being to remind us that we are straying
from the path which we, as Beings, chose to take—
our path from the Heart in the Light.

As Beings, before being incarnated in a material body, we knew how to take care of what was going to be our new vehicle. We felt sure and powerful in the knowledge that every time the people we were embodying strayed from their paths, we would be able to communicate with them through warnings of different intensities. First, we would send them light signals or warnings. If these were not enough for them to resume their paths, we would send them a more intense warning, such as a physical discomfort or a slight illness that would remind them to stop and readjust their course.

Provided we listen to them, illness or distress are warnings that permit us to re-establish contact with our inner selves, allowing us to see what it is wrong in what we are doing, what we are thinking, or the decisions we are making.

The problem lies in the fact that the incarnated person stops heeding the voice of her Knowledge. She forgets it! She no longer recognizes the signals and warnings. Ignorant of the meaning of the messages, people try to silence them, at least temporarily, with a visit to the doctor or a string of pills.

Although it is true that natural remedies like homeopathy or herbal supplements are used as less aggressive approaches compared with conventional pharmaceuticals, in the majority of cases people try to relieve the symptoms without recognizing their true meaning and importance.

It's just like the passenger in the taxi who cannot make himself heard by the driver, and seeing that the car keeps straying from its path and will not reach its destination, screams louder and louder trying to make himself heard. In this case, the Being, seeing itself increasingly removed from its path, will send us messages of ever greater intensity, which will be translated into distress, discomforts, blows, falls, accidents, and in the worst cases, serious illnesses.

Aging Does Not Mean Illness

Have you noticed how the older people get, the more discomfort and distress they experience? Our bodies are not designed by nature to manifest themselves in this way. With the passing years, they may begin to slow down and wear out, but the pain and distress that the majority of people suffer as they grow older is another thing altogether.

Bad digestion, aching joints, loss of vision, bowel movement problems, loss of flexibility, circulation problems, increases in blood sugar levels, high cholesterol, hypertension, premature hair loss, chronic fatigue, sleeping disorders, memory problems, and so forth—these are all symptoms that, although considered normal and chalked up to the passing years, in reality should not arise in a healthy and centered adult.

As we add years to our human lives, the Being sees itself increasingly powerless to keep the promises it made to itself. As a result, it tries to make itself heard with ever greater urgency. This, compounded by our poor diets and neglect of our bodies, is the reason these problems tend to increase with age.

Many of the older people I've worked with say they now feel lighter, healthier, and freer from distress compared with how they felt years ago, including in their youth or even in their childhood.

REMEMBER: Good health is the natural state of the organism. Illness, although it has become the norm for humans, is not natural. Note that I'm not saying that every warning from the Being is unnatural, such as gastroenteritis or a headache or a flu; I'm saying that they are warnings, not random or inevitable illnesses that it is our lot to suffer.

The Network of Interconnections in Our Body

As the energy Beings that we are, the energy that circulates in our bodies is organized in something like energy channels. Just like in a roundabout, there are points where the channels intersect, and it is vital that all the energy circulates harmoniously.

When this is not the case, the energy stagnates and distress sets in. Acupuncture and kinesiology have studied these energy channels in our bodies and have learned to unblock them to prevent the onset of illnesses.

However, simply unblocking these channels without getting to the root of the emotional causes of these blockages—that is, without recognizing the message that our Being is trying to transmit to us—would only serve to alleviate the pain temporarily not cure it.

Certain ancient cultures, such as the Chinese, studied the symbolism underlying physical symptoms. They gathered, observed, and classified the symbolic messages of distress in every part of the body. In this way, every instance of distress or pain traced to a certain location in our body corresponds to a specific emotion and a type of behavior.

Do you recall the case of Ruth who was suffering from gum disease? In general, gum problems are linked to intense anger or frustration that has remained repressed. Ruth's Being was trying to show her that she needed to release this anger and learn to forgive; to forgive others and herself for all the harm that had been inflicted on her in the past and the harm that she was still inflicting on herself. It was when Ruth began to free herself from these emotions that her gums began to heal, freeing her and her communication from her pain.

Eric's parents divorced when he was two years old. From then on he lived with his mother who proceeded to manipulate his reality so that he would come to hate and reject his father. His mother had been so insistent, Eric had not seen his father since he was ten years old. When Eric came to see me, at age forty, he had severe myopia, which was worsening despite his age. Since his childhood, Eric had been convinced that his father was akin to a monster who had abandoned him and his mother and had no interest in him whatsoever.

In our second session, he realized that maybe, just maybe, the reality that had been instilled in him by his mother, which he had then perpetuated and allowed to guide his emotional life, was not really what he thought it was. He resolved to speak to his father to express all the pain that he felt at being abandoned and ignored.

Eric could not have been more surprised to meet a kind, loving man, tormented by the time he had not shared with his son. They spent five long hours talking about all that had happened. His father explained that when Eric was a child, he had said that he didn't love his father and never wanted to see him again. He even showed him a letter in which Eric had wrote that he didn't want to have to visit him again.

Eric was stunned. He couldn't remember any of this. Blind to his reality, Eric had spent the better part of his life experiencing things through a skewed vision of reality. It took him a while to forgive his mother and re-establish a healthy relationship with his father, but as he did so his sight began to improve. Today it has improved enormously. He still needs glasses, but his perspective on life and relationships has changed altogether because he has finally stopped being the victim of his parents.

For Eric, the consequence of years of not listening to the signals of his Being and refusing to see reality is a simple myopia, but for others the effects of not being mindful of the messages conveyed by their Being can be much more serious and more painful, both in physical and emotional terms.

How important it is, then, to teach children to know the body they inhabit, as well as its functions and needs, and offer them an education with and from our Hearts, which will allow them to always remember the significance of their physical pains or symptoms of distress. With these tools, children will have everything they need to realize when they have created particular physical conditions in their lives through mistaken decisions and know how to find their way back to the path of well-being.

Sara, my friend Victoria's daughter, was only five months old when I met her. Even before learning to talk or to walk, when she saw me she would use her tiny fingers to point out which points on her body she wanted me to unblock. Until the age of two she would still run up to me, showing me the points that she needed me to work on and unblock, but from that age onward, she was already beginning to lose communication with her Being.

Not infrequently, when people who participate in my seminars or in individual sessions succeed in improving their relationship with themselves and others, they greatly improve their health in the process. They no longer have to use glasses, get rid of insomnia, free themselves from allergies, lose weight, improve their digestion, even overcome certain cancers and other severe physical ailments—all thanks to reconnecting with themselves and their Reality.

Human Nature is Addictive

The human body is a child of the Earth. Have you stopped to notice how planet Earth is in fact brimming with needs? Rain to prevent droughts;

trees and vegetation to protect it from the blazing rays of the sun and to clean the air that circulates on its surface; the light and heat of the sun so that its inhabitants may thrive and its surface remain inhabitable; maintaining the constant balance of its ecosystem, which regulates the number of Beings that can inhabit it; and many other needs besides.

Just like the Earth, mother of our bodies, we humans too are full of needs that control and limit our daily lives. If we wish to survive, we need to breathe, drink, eat, move, interact, feel recognized, feel loved, and many things besides.

The needs that physically control our lives create in us a perfect breeding ground for addictions, both physical and mental. Whether we are conscious of it or not, we all live with some type of addiction that, to a greater or lesser extent, limits our lives. Of all these addictions, it is the mental and emotional ones that, by their very subtlety, are the most difficult to identify and therefore to cure.

Addictions are ways of trying to feel something when we are suffering from an emotional emptiness, when we allow the darkness to set in deeply and flood us inwardly. Human beings, plagued by guilt, cling to addictions in order to evade reality, attempting not to see and not to think about what is going wrong. It is akin to a continuous suicide, the hope that life will pass and that this sense of meaninglessness she is experiencing day after day, disconnected as she is from her Essence, comes to an end.

If there is a common factor linking all forms of addiction that afflict human beings, it is the search for instant gratification and the avoidance of a painful emotion or sensation. In addiction to food, it is the pleasure of eating. In gambling, it is the rush of adrenaline produced by the risk of losing one's entire fortune. In drug addiction, it is the temporary pleasurable sensations generated by the drugs. In the addiction to pharmaceuticals, it is the numbing of oneself, the avoidance of pain or malaise, or the attainment of a state of contentment. Addiction is about escaping or hiding from oneself instead of finding a solution.

The problem that underlies any type of addictive behavior is that, as pleasurable as the immediate sensations may be, the medium and long-term results are invariably damaging: illness, bankruptcy, obesity, stress, family breakups, physical and mental breakdowns, and so on.

Addictions to smoking, drugs, gambling, pharmaceuticals, certain foods, eating, drinking, video games or even to people are so common nowadays that they have come to appear "normal" to us. And as if this predicament were not disheartening enough, now we have social networks, internet, computers, tablets, and cell phones to further facilitate this escape from reality and from oneself that addictions engender. For a large part of the population, cell phones have become the "perfect" form of escaping the present, of killing time without being aware of what is going on around them. The human being is like a country at war—occupied.

Re-establish Contact with Your Being to Recover and Strengthen Your Total Health

Asleep and unconscious to themselves, human beings live anesthetized. It's as if their lucidity, sensations, and emotions had been put to sleep or slowed down. A person immersed in her ignorance no longer feels, or does so to a limited degree. This lack of feeling is what triggers addictions and leaves people at the mercy of sects or whoever decides to manipulate them.

As I never tire of insisting, it is important that we be present, attend to our well-being, and nurture our genuine Reality so that we may be present to manifest our Love and enhance our Light (Evolution) every moment of our lives.

The moment you recognize the passenger that you carry in your inner taxi, there will no longer be room for addictions, or less room for them, and any cult or group intent on manipulation loses its influence over you. Once this happens, you no longer feel the need to escape your reality or seek out sensations through harmful forms of behavior.

One out of every five Americans is on medication for some kind of mental disorder! This is a clear sign that it is time to change course, recognize the passenger we are carrying inside, and remember Who we are. In this way, we reclaim our Power, which is nothing other than the echo of the infinite Power of our Creating Parents.

Epidemics, cancer, allergies and other autoimmune disorders—how much pain do you think you could spare yourself by getting back in touch with our Parents. The moment we recover trust in Life itself, in the Light of our Hearts, eternal co-creators of the All, we again feel eternally Alive!

The Great Nutritional Chaos

This planet is a far-flung orchard. It offers us everything we could possibly wish for perfect health and a fit body.

Look for a moment at the type of food that most people in "advanced" countries consume. The majority eat highly processed and modified foods that are far from beneficial to their health. Why do you think the food industry creates these highly processed and flavored foods? Once more, it is a case of satisfying the human body's need to experience intense and immediate sensations. They insert flavor enhancers and additives to make the texture more pleasurable, softer, crunchier, and crispier so that people will continue consuming them time and time again.

The food industry is very attuned to the addictive nature of human beings and offers them exactly what they are looking for: foods that give them intense feelings and for a moment allow them to forget everything else.

But is this what our bodies need to maintain our health and vitality? As human beings we are designed to nourish ourselves with food from the earth as we find it in nature or in a slightly modified form, such as cooked, fermented, dehydrated, and so forth.

The foods we eat, just like our bodies, are made of energy. Some are refreshing and therefore suitable for warmer periods; others are neutral and can be consumed throughout the year; and still others generate warmth and should be eaten in the colder seasons. In every season, the earth offers us the foods in tune with the climate experienced at that time of year.

You would never eat a piping hot soup in mid-summer when the heat is stifling. Why then do most people eat bananas, tomatoes, and other warm weather foods all year long? The quantity of eating options available nowadays, and the sheer number of diets and theories on food in general, is so vast that people end up seriously confused.

While you re-establish contact with your Being and become more sensitive to the real physical needs of your vehicle, you can use the following simple guidelines:

- Eat organic products that are in season and, if possible, raised locally. (Remember the importance of having enough money?)
- Eliminate all refined foods—everything that contains white sugar or white flour.
- Eliminate or at least reduce your intake of cow's milk and related products.
- Eliminate conventional wheat, which is nothing more than a hybrid that is difficult to digest and harmful to your intestines and general health.
- Incorporate lots of beans, seeds, and vegetables, seasonal fruits, and proteins of your choice into your diet.

For more, stay posted. I am very interested in the natural and conscious care of the body and am currently writing a book on the subject with my friend and writer Victoria Vinuesa, who is an expert in this area.

Physical Exercise

The human body is made to be in motion. Physical exercise is not only fundamental to the health and well-being of our bodies but also to our Happiness.

Can we be happy in a damaged or stricken vehicle? It's as if the taxi driver in our analogy hopes to enjoy the drive in a car that is leaking oil or has punctured tires—without a doubt the experience would not be as pleasant as it would be in a smoothly running car.

When I speak of physical exercise, I don't mean going to the gym, running, and working out intensely. I mean a light form of exercise that is easy on the body. In my experience, the most beneficial exercises that can be practiced daily, after walking, are yoga, some form of martial art, swimming, dancing, rowing, zip lines, and rock climbing; all are unaggressive sports that can be done year round. Suffering in a gym to attain a good-looking body according to given social criteria, apart from being highly addictive, is neither natural nor does it increase your health.

Contact with Nature

The human body is an offspring of the earth and needs frequent contact with it. If your aim is to be healthy and happy, you will need frequent contact with Nature; that is, with trees, water, soil, wind, and the sounds and silences that Nature has to offer.

Let me offer you an experience. Close your eyes, breathe deeply, and try to smell the fragrances of the forest in the first days of autumn when the weather begins to grow colder and the moisture from the first rains brings out the scents of the soil. Listen to the songs of birds as they fly from branch to branch. Feel the majestic presence of the trees. Now tell me: What does it make you feel? In general, my students respond with a sigh of satisfaction and longing, accompanied by a peaceful smile.

Our bodies, continually surrounded by and exposed to electromagnetic waves of all types in the environment, need to regain their natural balance; in other words, they need to release the electricity that has built up in their cells. It is precisely by regularly coming into direct contact with the soil and the natural elements that we can achieve this.

If you live in a city that is predominantly paved, first consider changing your lifestyle. In the meantime, try taking off your shoes and socks every time you get home and feeling the floor beneath your feet. When you go to bed, turn off the Wi-Fi for yourself and for your family, so that, at least during the night, you can breathe and rest without being surrounded by damaging electromagnetic waves. If possible, ask your neighbors to do the same.

REMEMBER: There are a thousand ways to get in touch with Nature in our daily lives. Go and discover yours.

CHAPTER 29

You Promised Yourself to Care for the Planet

The Earth is a dual Being, illuminated by the light of the Sun and surrounded by darkness. As such, it wants to be illuminated.

Planet Earth, like all the planets floating in our universal space, is itself a Being—a Being with its share of darkness and Light. As a Being in evolution, it therefore needs interaction with other Beings.

Like you or I, the Earth needs to be loved and respected and likes to enjoy our peace and Happiness. Although it doesn't generate its own light, this precious planet that shelters you and I needs to feel the gratitude of its "children," of us, the people who inhabit it. We all interact daily with the Earth, a Being that for us is such a huge entity.

Through Their Daily Acts, Human Beings Have Long Made It Clear That They Are Mainly Destructive, and Are So Naturally

Earth provides us with everything we could possibly want or need. But as human beings, we dedicate ourselves to destroying it a little at a time, now more than ever.

We cut down its trees without replanting them and destroy its vegetation. We contaminate its air with our factories and conventional cars. We contaminate its rivers and seas with pesticides, nuclear waste, detergents, and other toxins. We upset its delicate ecosystem. We modify the genetic structure of its crops and trees. We destroy the ozone layer that protects it from the intense rays of the sun with our irresponsible use of air conditioning. We disrupt its surface with fracking and other aggressive technologies, and so on.

It's as if you had millions of lice in your hair, tearing your hair out, dumping their trash on you, making noise, spilling poison, shaving your hair to make room for streets and houses, throwing firecrackers on you, and excavating your scalp.

Imagine that a friend lends you her house so that can spend your vacation there. Would you proceed to destroy it, make it dirty, and modify it for the sake of your temporary comfort? No, of course not! It would be reasonable to assume that you would make sure to leave it just as you found it. You might even leave behind an extra decoration or an appliance as a gesture of gratitude.

This planet is like that holiday house that is lent to us for a limited amount of time.

Human Beings Must Keep Their Promises

One of the promises we made to ourselves in embarking on this human experience was to take care of the planet hosting us. So why did we proceed to destroy the house we inhabit? Having forgotten Who they are and what this temporary earthly experience truly represents for their Creator Father-Mother, human beings selfishly try to enjoy this life to the utmost, believing it to be the only one.

Time and again, human beings seek to enrich themselves at all costs, without thinking of the consequences for the health of the planet and future generations. They simply don't care. In their ignorance, they become coldly insensitive, and in extreme cases cannot distinguish right from wrong. They act purely for their own benefit, which they confuse with Happiness, and naturally they neglect that Being, mother of their bodies, on which they live and which they only see as nothing more than a plot of land they can possess.

Doesn't it seem absurd that we should want to appropriate a plot of land as if it were ours and we could take it with us when we are gone?

Ecology Is Not a Trend But a Need Created By Us As a Result of Mistreating the Planet

Admittedly, ecological changes must be made on a scale beyond our individual lives; nevertheless, each of us can do his part to stop the destruction of a planet that gives us everything and asks for very little in return until the hour of our departure, when we give it our bodies.

If the majority of Western populations refused to consume foods teeming with noxious pesticides and, instead, demanded cleaner crops, producers would have no choice but to offer healthier alternatives. If we refused to buy air conditioners and refrigerators that damage the ozone layer, or didn't use cleaning products that are toxic for the environment and for us, don't you think that science would be evolved enough to find healthy and non-destructive alternatives?

If we refused to buy clothes, food, and all other types of products that are imported from distant countries and, instead, demanded local products that haven't traveled thousands of miles to get here, we could have a positive impact on the reduction of air pollution, and in the process, curb the exploitation of the people and environment of underdeveloped countries. If we were to no longer buy cars that run on fossil fuels, wouldn't we be forced to use other less polluting means?

By refusing to use dangerous and, above all, unnecessary nuclear energy, governments would have no choice but to offer cleaner, less harmful alternatives. It's not a question of science inventing new methods for generating electricity; those methods already exist! They have already been invented, but their commercial potential has not yet been explored.

We all have the power to choose between continuing our daily abuse of the planet or treating it with the care it deserves; to recognize and be thankful for all that it offers us each day; to love it like the mother of our body that it truly is.

Re-Establish Contact With the Elements

The elements on this planet—wind, water, fire, and earth—are also Beings. Therefore, learn to love them and communicate with them.

Part Five

Make Peace With Death
And Enjoy Your Life

CHAPTER 30

Death as a Continuation
of Your Path

Many of us are taught from birth that this life is the only one we are going to have. In Reality, your Life is eternal and multidimensional. Believing that Life is confined to this human experience is reductionist.

Over the centuries, different societies, religions, and power groups have instilled in us the belief that Life only exists here on Earth. The belief of many was that if you behaved well, according to the criteria of a given institution, you would attain eternal life in a place called heaven, or paradise, or something of that nature. According to others, you would gradually attain the necessary "perfection" over the course of several lives, different reincarnations on this same planet, and only then would you be allowed into something resembling the heaven of others.

But what if, in Reality, we were much greater and more complex than that? What if our Life continues in different bodies of varying solidity, in different places in the universe, as well as in different universes?

You—that is, your Being—have been evolving for an eternity, passing from one form to another, from one place to another, and still have an eternity to enjoy this evolution toward more Loving places, where well-being is the rule and suffering the exception. To do this your Being will increasingly use light bodies adapted to the density of those worlds where well-being is more easily attainable, free from the limits imposed by society, such as gender, class, creed, or the color of one's skin.

Do you dare to imagine it? What Happiness! What a thrill! What an adventure!

There was once a nomad, an eternal traveler, who one day arrived in a seaside town. A friend had lent him his house so that he could spend a few days enjoying the pleasures of the sea and fresh air before going on to his next destination.

The nomad, excited to discover a new place, went for a stroll on the beach. Barefoot, he began walking on the stunning white sand. The water was bathing his feet when suddenly he was shrouded in a dense fog. With great difficulty, blinded by the fog, he managed to find his way back to the house and fell into a deep slumber from which he didn't wake until noon the following day.

Bewildered and confused, he couldn't remember where he was or why he was there. He got out of bed and resolved to make some repairs to the house that now was the center of his life. He spent the entire day rearranging the furniture, painting the walls a different color, cutting several trees so that they would no longer block the view from the windows, and even put tiles over the grass that led to the house.

A week passed and the nomad had not left the house that he now considered his, the only one for him, the only house that existed or could ever exist.

His friend, concerned about his odd behavior, went to speak with him. He tried to bring him to his senses so that he could continue on his path, but the nomad no longer recognized him and bolted the doors and windows to stop anyone from taking him away.

A few months later he received a letter from his friend's lawyer: charges had been brought against him to force him to leave the house. The tormenting thought that, at any time, they might come and take him away from "his home," indeed from his entire life, didn't allow him to get any sleep. He spent every day and night watching television or busied himself with countless tasks simply trying not to think about it, trying to forget that the end might arrive at any moment.

The fateful day arrived and the nomad, devastated, was removed by force from the house which, for the last few months, had been his entire universe. Several men were required to carry him out of his refuge.

Once outside, however, an intense ray of sunlight touched his slumbering heart. Suddenly, everything within him was illuminated, as if he had woken from a nightmare, and his memory came flooding back. He remembered who He was, he remembered the boundless joy that his nomadic life brought him, his constant travels and discoveries, his constant awakenings and growth. He could not help crying out of joy at the sight of his sympathetic friend who was now waiting for him with open arms.

Just like this nomad, the human being confuses this experience on Earth, which he likes to call "life," with real Life, which in itself is thrilling and eternal. Just like the nomad who was forced to leave his temporary refuge, the human being, knowing that sooner or later he will have to return his body—an act that he calls "dying"—feels anguish and fear. His life is filled with anxiety and stress, and he feels that his time is passing too quickly, that life is running through his fingers. He decides to have kids to perpetuate himself, in order to feel that, in some sense, at least, he will continue to exist through them.

A very common phrase among the elderly who are approaching the time to leave their body is, "If I had known then what I know now, my life would have been totally different."

Death as Celebration

Death is an act of celebration of the fact that the Being, its missions accomplished, decides to continue on the eternal path of evolution. The problem lies in the fact that the majority of Beings depart without having concluded their earthly mission, and that the way they choose to leave their body is often accompanied by suffering, pain, and many regrets.

Valerie was a nurse and at the age of forty-five had only a few days left to live. She was suffering from terminal cancer, which had spread throughout her body. The doctors had sent her home so that she could die surrounded by her family. When she came to my office, she could hardly walk. Her husband and nephew were holding her up while she came in, to prevent her legs from buckling. Her husband went to sit in the waiting room, fearing she would not be able to make it through the session.

Valerie was devastated. Although she accepted her illness and her suffering, she had a tremendous fear of being buried or cremated and was afraid of leaving her body in spite of all the suffering it had caused her.

During the session, Valerie understood why this painful illness had been created and the message that her Being had attempted to convey to her. She forgave and freed herself from the heavy burden of guilt, resentment, and anguish that had plagued her all her life. The relief that she experienced in remembering the Reality of her Life in her own eternity was such that when she left, radiant and grateful, her husband could not believe it.

Before the end of that one and only meeting I had with her, Valerie told me that now she felt ready and even thrilled about carrying on her journey. But she told me that something still caused her pain, like a thorn in her side: she felt hurt that her son, now twenty years old, had never hugged her.

A week later, at her home and surrounded by family, Valerie felt nauseated and her husband took her to the bathroom because she was going to be sick. She asked him to leave her alone for a moment. Suddenly she got very dizzy, and abruptly she felt a pair of strong arms around her shoulders, catching her before she fell. It was her son. Valerie departed this world cradled in her son's embrace, which she had yearned for for so long.

She had expressed the wish that her loved ones celebrate her departure with a party. Her friends and colleagues spoke affectionately of the great tenderness her eyes had conveyed in the days before her passing. They said that a change had come over her, something that served them as an example of courage. Valerie passed on happily, from her recovered Heart and recovered communication with her Being.

The Light of Your Heart Is the Only Fuel You Need to Get Back on the Path Home

Valerie had increased her luminous capital in the last few days of her life, after returning to her Being and finally understanding her great mistake—a mistake that had caused her to develop cancer in order to help end her life here, despite being married and having a child on this Earth.

This luminous capital—that is, the light that she had allowed herself to radiate through her experience—served as fuel to travel from this universe to other more luminous worlds, resonating with her new vibration. But as we've discussed, in most cases, people, connected to their egos, do not increase their luminous capital enough to depart when the time comes. At that juncture they must decide: to incarnate themselves once more in a human body or to wait in the form of an atomic body until they have increased their Light enough to continue their journey.

For me, it has been natural to co-exist on a daily basis with these atomic bodies of Beings who have decided to illuminate themselves instead of being reincarnated. Ever since I can remember, every time I have perceived these atomic bodies I have understood that we are inhabiting a space that is just as much theirs as it is ours, even though human beings don't allow themselves to see or perceive them.

When I was a child, I would spend long hours in the woods of Bordeaux. There, sheltered by the towering trees, enveloped by my good friend the wind, stroked by the mild rain, and cradled by the leaves and grass, I would spend hours alone, surrounded by those silent beings in evolution.

One day—I must have been around six at the time—I was sitting on the trunk of an old fallen tree, when the atomic body of what had once been a woman conveyed to me that she was there because during her life she had hardly used her Heart. She explained how, during her human life, she had ignored her innermost feelings. The woman she had once been had not allowed herself to achieve what she wanted to achieve nor had listened closely enough to know what could have made her happy. She had simply "functioned." She spoke of the inexhaustible Love that we all have inside us and without which nobody could even exist. She said that nothing is worth doing without Love.

We used to meet each day in that forest and would share long moments of affectionate silence. One particular day, when I had been punished for freeing the birds from our neighbor's cage once again, I felt a strong desire to feel her presence, but to my surprise I did not find her. I searched and called out to her, but she wasn't there. Sadness overwhelmed me, and I fell asleep against the tree trunk.

When I woke up, it was dark and there was my friend, sitting next to me. My ghost friend explained that what needed freedom, even more than my neighbor's canaries, was the luminous child that lived inside me and needed me in order to feel liberated and loved. She suggested that I use my Heart in whatever I did or thought and that I should have lots of fun. That I should give myself all the attention that I could and do all that was in my power to protect myself from harmful situations—especially those caused by myself—which I might encounter and which could cause me suffering or lead me to hide from myself.

I listened to her attentively, and on that occasion she appeared much more luminous than usual. The distant barking of a dog reminded me that if I didn't want to risk more punishment, I needed to leave quickly. When I left her that night I felt immensely grateful. Although I could not touch her with my material body, I did feel her intense embrace and great emotion.

That night I dreamed of her. She was strikingly luminous, and for the first time, she was smiling happily. All of the atoms of her luminous body glowed with intense lights and vibrant colors. We had met in the woods as always, but this time we were standing and facing each other. She revealed to me that after a wait of fifty years in terrestrial time, finally she had enough light to continue on her path and embark on a new life in the beyond. This time she had made herself a solemn promise to live fully and harmoniously, with herself as well as with the world that she was now preparing to incorporate herself into. A gentle stroke awakened me from that wonderful dream. Opening my eyes, I saw her disappearing before me. I never saw her again in the forest, or anywhere else.

Remember the message of this already lucid Being. Always listen to the voice of your Heart, enjoy yourself and be happy to the utmost, allow yourself to feel, love yourself, and take care of yourself. The sooner we understand this and put it into practice, the sooner we can start bringing Happiness in our lives, the less we will fear the moment of departure, and the more fuel we will have at our disposal to travel to other more luminous worlds.

The more Light you generate, the more luminous will be the place you choose. To put it in simplistic terms, it's like someone intending to buy a house. She will not have the same options if she has $10 million dollars as if she has $200,000 or $10,000.

Boost your luminous capital by authorizing yourself to enjoy life.

CHAPTER 31

Your Life is Multidimensional

One of the most common causes of suffering I know results from the age-old belief of many populations that our life only exists here on Earth. In fact, as Beings, we experience multiple Lives and don't belong to any specific place, even though we are now experiencing a life on planet Earth.

Let me offer you an image that will help you dispel this myth.

Try to visualize your tiny body on the immense planet that you inhabit, then imagine the miniscule Earth in relation to the Sun, which is a million times bigger. Now visualize how small the Sun is relative to the size of our galaxy, the Milky Way. Small, right? Finally, consider how tiny our galaxy is when compared with the entire universe. Now, what if I asked you to take one more step and visualize how relatively miniscule our universe is next to the infinite number of universes that co-exist in the same space?

Now that you have felt, at least for a brief moment, how infinitely tiny you and planet Earth are physically in relation to the immensity of Creation, doesn't it seem absurd and reductionist to think that there is life only on this infinitesimal point in the universe?

The problem, as always, lies in the fact that we identify ourselves with our physical bodies and our personal history, not with the eternal Beings that we are. We cannot imagine living anywhere else but this earthly planet, adapted to this human body, which is in itself a child of the Earth. Where do you think this belief comes from, the ego or the Heart?

REMEMBER: Limitations always come from the already limited ego-mind.

There, Where the Heart Prevails

According to my perception of Reality, many parallel planes co-exist at the same time in the same universe. On this planet we inhabit, there are various co-existing realities—other worlds, other realities, other Beings, and other experiences that practically nobody is conscious of or perceives.

Just as various dimensions co-exist in this universe, so too do an infinite number of universes, superimposed on each other, sharing the space we call "infinite."

To the human mind, Reality is unimaginable.

Nevertheless, science is beginning to corroborate this Reality. There isn't only one universe, but an infinite number of them. The good news is that the majority of these universes are more luminous, and the Heart prevails to a greater extent than the universe in which we now are temporarily living. These are universes where Well-being, Love, Joy, Health, Beauty, Abundance, and Kindness prevail—universes where it is much easier to plug into a luminous current than to a dark one.

But the myriad options don't end there, because just as there are an infinite number of universes more luminous than the one we inhabit, in this very universe there are an infinite number of places more luminous than planet Earth.

Have you ever considered the fact that Earth is a planet that doesn't emit light of its own? It is dark, dense, and solid, with an immense core of fire, and it floats in darkness. Earth needs the external light of the stars to offer us a sense of scale.

Doesn't it seem extraordinary to finally realize that you have the possibility of constructing your present and future experience—an experience that can lead you to where you will feel infinitely better, freer, and happier?

Your earthly experience will determine to which place in this or other universes you will be able to travel. The choice is yours in each instant. Choose your Heart!

We Are Manifold

Just as there are infinite external possibilities to experience, there are infinite possibilities inside us; that is, in our internal universe. As Beings, we carry within us an infinite universe of possible experiences.

Be multiple! These were the words of a great wise man (from the knowledge of his Heart) who visited this planet many centuries ago. "Be multiple," he said. The words of that wise man were interpreted and translated by some institutions to their own benefit as "multiply," in the sense of having children who could then be made into our subjects.

We exist to have a multiplicity of different experiences over the course of this life, and each subsequent one that we choose to experience. Consider for a moment our manifold reality already manifest. We are sons and fathers, brothers and friends, daughters and mothers, sisters and friends, employees and bosses, students and teachers, we obey and command, learn and instruct, laugh and cry, work and rest, sleep and awaken, we are born and die.

We were born into this human realm to experience ourselves from the multiplicity of our possibilities. The richness of life lies therein. The more experiences you allow yourself to live through the Light of your own Heart, the more options to enjoy them you will create.

The richer your experiences, the more possibilities you will have of evolving through them. The courage of those who dare to keep their promises, to live instead of survive, to live from their Heart, is the happy result of allowing oneself to be a child of the Light.

Imagine two middle-aged women, both with children, who live in the same town and are married to two men who have the same profession. The first is a woman who is loving, cheerful, social with her neighbors, has good friends, and is open and creative. Every morning, she goes walking through a nearby forest with her friends. Twice a week, she participates in yoga classes in a neighboring town. Together with her husband, she enjoys pleasant evening get-togethers with all of her friends. She is taking singing lessons and has joined a group that rehearses together every Saturday. She takes care of her children, and the time she spends with them she enjoys fully. They go to the movies, museums, galleries, concerts and artistic performances.

The second woman spends most of her time at home, cooking out of obligation, for her children and husband. Although she complains, she is constantly worrying about what they are doing or not doing, to the point that they begin to feel stifled. Their relationship is tense and joyless. The only time this woman leaves the house is when she has to go shopping. She hardly has friends and prefers to spend her time at home, where she feels protected from danger. It's easy to see which of these two women treats herself more kindly.

The first chooses to live her life in myriad different forms, all rooted in her Heart. The forms she chooses increase her chances of interacting, feeling, sharing, and evolving in the process. The second, patently less loving toward herself, removes herself from life and from others in order to keep surviving, and cuts off all communication in the process. She isolates herself in the false security of her home. The experiences she creates from her lack of self-Love are monotonous and routine, offering her scant possibilities of illuminating her darkness. At the same time, the sadness and boredom that her choices provoke in her keep her in the ever-painful position of the victim, envious and critical of everything others do.

REMEMBER: Action focused from the peace of the Heart creates success and promotes growth. Inactivity, monotony, and routine arise from fear; they immobilize and stymie the natural evolution of our Beings.

Dare to be manifold. Dare to interact with others and enjoy yourself.

CHAPTER 32

Enjoy Your Life

*Happiness is for those who dare to fill their lives
with their Hearts and determination.*

The perfect time to make changes, to improve the path of your life, is always the present. But many people postpone the moment of their own Happiness, simply waiting for something to happen or stop happening.

Now that you know the keys to attaining Happiness in your daily life, how long are you going to wait to begin manifesting it? How long will you put off spreading the light from your Light and your total well-being? How long will you wait to allow yourself to feel happy, thus becoming the Success of your life?

Many of the students I've met in the more than twenty years I've spent engaged in this wonderful profession have given me excuses for continuing to be lost and not being happy. All of them expect something to happen that would allow them to be happy:

"Once I get a new house," "Once I find the partner of my dreams," "Once I lose weight," "Once my kids grow up," "Once I get rid of these allergies," "Once I find a job," "Once I earn more money," "Once I solve my financial problems," "Once I fix my marriage," "Once I find the courage to leave my partner," "Once my child recovers from his illness," "Once there is a change in government," "Once my father learns to love me," "Once I have a new boss," "Once my kids respect me," "Once I get rid of this cellulite," "Once I get my nose redone," "Once I get married," "Once I have children," "Once I retire," "Once I finish paying off my mortgage," "Once I find new friends," "Once I complete my studies," "Once there's no more suffering in this world."

Once, once, once...

You want these "once" to arrive, don't you? Then the first step is to feel happy because of who you are, because you are eternal, because you are infinitely and unconditionally loved by your Parents, because you still have so much Beauty to discover and Love to share, because your heart beats, because you don't just have an ego that makes you get lost, because you still have so many good loved ones and places to discover and share Who you are with, because the invaluable gift of being loved that has been given to you by Our Parents has been given to you Always, because you are a generator of Love and a motor of Happiness, because in your Heart there is illusion and tenderness, intelligence, and great creativity, and so on…

The list of reasons to feel Happiness is never-ending. So, stop delaying and realize, once and for all, who *is* your Creator Father-Mother.

Choose to flow from your Reality, and let yourself flow with an energy current of well-being that allows you to climb levels in every aspect, including economically, and become who you have always been and forever will be. Feeling happy is what will allow you to create and attract more well-being to your day-to-day existence, not hiding from others, from rules, from the fear of not having the right ability.

Do yourself a favor: stop waiting.

Live Your Life to Its Utmost Possibilities

Allow yourself to enjoy things from this precise moment onward. Live your life as if each day were your last one on the face of this planet.

Remember that the more you permit yourself to be the main actor in the present moment, the more enjoyment you will be generating for your short-term and long-term future, both in this world and future ones that you will visit.

Make being happy your first and foremost daily duty. Alone at home or on the street, smile on life, smile with no fear.

Your life, Life, is greater than anything you've ever dared to imagine. Its Beauty is infinite; its Well-being and its Love have no end.

Allow Yourself to Change Perspective

Human beings have a tendency to take things for granted. They assume that the planet they inhabit is theirs; the bodies they use are theirs; the house, the car, and all the things and tools they use on a daily basis are theirs; and that their children, their parents, and their partners are theirs.

In fact, these have all been created by the Essence and belong to the mother of their bodies: Earth.

Feeling grateful is both a marvelous and powerful act of acknowledgment and humility that, without a doubt, increases and spreads your Love. Give thanks for all that this life offers you and for all you've already been able to Love, co-create, and enjoy, no matter how little it may seem to you.

Give thanks for the fact that you're reading this book, for having drawn it into your path, for taking an important step toward your awakening and evolution.

REMEMBER: Your body, the one with which you have identified for so long, is nothing more than your vehicle. It is a child of the Earth, and the Earth will reclaim it once You decide to continue your path. You are not your body; you are much more than that. Beauty dwells within you. Thank your Parents, your Life. and yourself.

Dare!

We all have something hidden inside that we've always wanted to do or learn about but have never granted ourselves the chance to do so. It may be learning how to paint, play an instrument, visit another country, cook, sing, learn, dance, or some other passion.

Why not grant yourself a new opportunity to enjoy yourself and spread your Love and creativity? What are you waiting for? How long will you wait before embarking on a deliberate quest for the things that make you happy (Light)?

REMEMBER: Life is for those who Love it, discover it, and enrich themselves.

Move Up a Level

Changing course is a necessary step for anyone wanting to make any good and enriching change in their life. You cannot expect to continue doing what you've been doing and get different results. It just doesn't work that way.

Imagine for a moment that you spent years buying the same newspaper and didn't like its political orientation. Logically speaking, if you keep buying the same newspaper, you will continue to read news from the same political perspective that you do not endorse. Who is to blame if you keep reading it? Instead of waiting for the newspaper to change, make the change yourself. Switch newspapers. Act. Do something!

Until now you have been adhering to certain more or less rapid/slow and luminous/dark vibrational levels; those that you yourself have permitted yourself to experience and enjoy. This is the level in which you felt comfortable, to which you felt you belonged.

Now, and at any given moment, you may choose to increase your vibrational level from your awakened, or more awakened, Heart. You may choose to spread your Light and flow naturally and easily with richer and happier vibrational currents that will invariably bring more well-being into your life.

Your Life offers you the possibility, at each moment, to construct the experiences you yourself decide to live—the experience of any level of success, health, prosperity, or joy you could wish for. Imagine someone saying to you: If you dedicate yourself to being happy for one whole year, I will pay you a million dollars. What would you do? Well, Life works the same way.

REMEMBER: Your Life offers you everything. The only thing it asks for in return is that you be happy, that you enjoy yourself, and that you spread your Love.

CHAPTER 33

Global Consciousness

The human being is more afraid of his Heart (Light)
than his Ego (darkness).

Happiness and Well-Being exist in, and are available to, every human being inhabiting this planet. These beneficial states stand ever ready to manifest themselves through our every human act. But because we are closed to our pure and simple Reality, we simply choose not to spread Happiness and Well-Being. We are asleep.

Just as having a beautiful Rolls-Royce is useless if there's no one to drive it, or having an umbrella during a downpour is useless unless you choose to open it, so too merely having a Heart is not enough to guarantee a Happy and full life; you must choose to use it. Allow yourself, just for a moment, to open your eyes to Reality as it is. You will discover that each and every one of us is, in fact, solely responsible for ourselves and our choices in life. Common behaviors like judging others or worrying about what they are doing or not doing will suddenly seem absurd to you.

Imagine a very luminous Being on Its eternal universal journey making a short stop on Earth. It has decided not to incarnate itself here and has come just to observe us. From the Being's loving perspective, unencumbered by judgments and the limitations of the mind, It sees that the intelligence of the Heart no longer rules human beings.

It sees a group of people governed by the ego-mind of others, who, because of this, fight and kill each other in wars. It sees Beings who continually destroy the planet they inhabit, Beings who abuse and destroy others and themselves, Beings who are capable of hating or killing for the different names they attribute to God, or for their race or their sexual orientation. It sees that a deep-seated ignorance has taken control of a world created for manifesting Love and Happiness in harmony with the Heart that has created it.

It sees Beings who deem themselves superior due to the color of their skin, the family they belong to (or so they believe), and the country or social class they were born into.

It sees a multitude of Beings who, feeling alone and guilty, pay for their resentment with harsh criticism and judgment—Beings who are more concerned with the behavior of others than their own Evolution and Happiness, yet carry Tenderness and Kindness within them.

With compassion, It observes how the Beings who inhabit this planet have forgotten Who they are and what they have come here to do, their promises, their Parents, and therefore their own Heart.

God Is Pure Love

My Knowledge, which is the same as the Knowledge that resides in you, tells me that the God that humans don't talk about, or barely talk about, is pure Love.

God does not create sin to punish people, nor does He create a place called "hell" to burn evil people who have not behaved as He expects them to (for some reason humans assume that it's a he). Infinitely loving God, the Creating Essence Father-Mother, created all of us from Its infinite Love; we are part of It, and therefore It is within us.

The Essence is both Father and Mother of our Being.

The only thing that the Essence requests of us is that we manifest it, and that's only possible from the Heart, cradle of its Love in each of us.

When we err, it does not judge us—we already have ourselves for that; it simply expects us to resume our path back Home.

This Essence does not need to create sin to convince human beings to behave in a certain way; it only asks that they dedicate themselves to increasing the luminous intelligence that it has given them, the direct inheritance in their Hearts for the duration of their journeys through the so-called "eternity."

The Essence, as the Love and pure superior intelligence that it is, never judges or punishes you. It only Loves. Whosoever remains asleep to his true reason for existing, and is therefore lost and mistaken, is in most need of Love's look and compassion.

Sins and punishment are born of the human mind. Compassion, forgiveness, understanding, kindness, on the other hand, are and will always be offspring of the Essence.

Humans, blind to their Essence, created punishment and sins to control the population and prevent them from straying from the path they believed must be followed—a path that human minds believed must be followed so that things would adhere to an order they themselves had created.

If every one of your actions is guided by the infinite Light and intelligence of your Heart, you run no risk of "sinning" or straying from your path back Home. You only make mistakes while searching for the steps that will lead you back, and that's natural. It's what we call Evolution.

Making mistakes is inevitable, because you are a human being. You *will* make mistakes repeatedly, you *will* fall, as will those who accompany you. When this happens, simply follow the example of a baby beginning to walk: Get up and return to your path without looking back, one step at a time, using the rhythm of your Heart, and forgive yourself and others. This is what the Father and Mother Essence in you expects, if it expects anything at all.

REMEMBER: To err is human. The important thing is that you mend your ways, and that you love, time and again, wherever you may choose to go.

CHAPTER 34

Daring to Be Happy Means...
Choosing to Feel Happy

A promise is a debt. At the beginning of this book, I asked you to accompany me as we discovered why being daring is a task for the brave and a necessary step toward attaining Happiness. I'm sure that by now you will have glimpsed some, if not all, of the reasons for this.

To feel happy, or happier, you can choose to:

LOOK INSIDE YOURSELF: Being happy necessarily means daring to look at the passenger that you are carrying in the taxi. It means becoming, a little more each day, Who you are and Who you came to manifest.

ASSUME THE RESPONSIBILITY FOR YOUR OWN HAPPINESS: Feeling happy implies assuming responsibility for your own Life, realizing that you and only you are responsible for the care and expansion of your core of Love.

RECOGNIZE THAT YOU HAVE MADE A MISTAKE: Feeling happy means realizing and acknowledging that, for many years, you have been turning your back on yourself, turning your back, in a greater or lesser degree, on our Parents in you.

ACCEPT YOUR DUAL NATURE: Feeling happy means clearly seeing how you behave and accepting yourself as you are in this very moment. It means accepting that you are not perfect and that that is okay, as long you continue evolving at your own pace. It means accepting that your sole responsibility is to Love.

FORGIVE: Feeling happy means getting rid of the resentment that is paralyzing you and choosing forgiveness instead of vengeance. Forgiving liberates you. Contained vengeance and anger increase your ignorance.

FORGIVE YOURSELF: Once you've understood, accepted, and taken responsibility for your mistakes, it is vital that you forgive yourself for them. Your Parents do not judge you, so don't judge yourself.

REMEMBER: Guilt invariably seeks punishment. Feeling guilty will always lead you to harm yourself, both consciously and unconsciously. Your sole responsibility is to recognize and nurture yourself. Stop judging yourself. Choose to forgive yourself and forgive others. Don't forget that you, like others, were just mistaken.

LOVE AND ACCEPT YOURSELF AS YOU ARE: Feeling happy means daring to love yourself just as you are in this precise moment, in the midst of your evolution, with your flaws and virtues. Dare to look at yourself in the mirror and say without the least hesitation, "I love you, (say your name)."

TAKE CARE OF YOUR "VEHICLE" AND THE "HOUSE" IN WHICH YOU LIVE: Feeling happy means recognizing the vehicle (your body) and the house (Mother Earth) that have been granted to you to carry out your earthly experience. It means gratefully using these precious gifts you've been given by the Essence, your body, and Mother Earth and treating them with care, respect, and affection on a daily basis.

MAKE PEACE WITH THE LOVE THAT CREATED YOU: Feeling happy implies being able to once again look at Our Creating Parents of the All within You and being able to recognize the Love reflected in Its infinite gaze.

REMEMBER: You are not alone! You've never been alone! You will never be alone! Return to your own pace, without hurry, and without pause. But return.

Glossary

Alchemy: your Power to transform the darkness you cross into Light.

Love: God Father-Mother is the joyful Eternity, the chosen experienced Happiness. The space in which the good is possible.

Beauty: your loving inner space, expanding in your own way.

Well-Being: your inner space as it is free from conflicts between your ego and your Heart. A state of Peace.

Luminous Capital: the Love that you have used to enjoy and share over the course of your eternal journey.

Knowledge: your loving patrimony, intelligence in harmony with the one that created you. Your only guide.

Heart: cradle of Love. Residence of Our Parents (I am) in you. Principal and most powerful tool for co-creating. In the Heart resides the Knowledge (droplet of the Essence). It is the hidden Intelligence gifted to us by Our Parents.

Awakening: it is re-cognizing (accepting once again) the infinitely loving God, Father-Mother in you.

Ego: the motor of our evolution, unique to each person. It is the voice of ignorance (darkness) that surrounds your Being.

Emotion: a state that indicates, with total clarity, how your inner passenger feels, your Being.

Creating Essence: the source from which you are born; the droplet within you.

Evolution: return Home (God), accepting and correcting your daily errors.

Success: feeling happy and co-creating richness with illusion, determination, and humility.

Happiness: the fuel that allows us to travel freely through Eternity, if and only if we remember to fuel up at each stop.

Strength: it is linked to the will, and it is dark, demanding, and destined to exhaust itself.

Guide: Yourself. The harmonious union between your Identity and your personality.

Ignorance: lack of Love; vacuum of Love. To stray in pursuit of the power over others and knowledge.

Supreme Intelligence: pure Love. Another name for the Source of the All.

Inherent guilt: the manipulation of the ego over your mind and person, still asleep to its Reality. The wrong path for returning home.

The Source: the loving representation of God Father-Mother in each one of us.

Light: the droplet of the Essence in you; Knowledge. Your fuel for returning home and which you will increase thanks to the daily choices you make through your mission.

Inner master: your sole guide; the voice of your Heart.

Empowering Message: a thought chosen and used as a request to heal, enrich, and redirect your life.

Fear: the inner void that pushes you to seek Love. It is your best enemy.

Mission: the human manifestation of your purpose.

Natural vs. normal: Natural is born of Being; normal is born of society.

Forgetting: to be asleep to your Reality. To turn your back on your Eternity and your Heart, to our Parents.

Parents: the Creating Mother and Father Essence (the feminine and masculine in all that exists).

Power: the Love and its creative intelligence; a state that never fades but grows in you and is never exhausted.

Purpose: it is born of Being and consists in evolving (manifesting Love on the path back Home) in each instant. It is Being's objective.

The Being: the "I" that inhabits the body. It is the free will in each of us, always between the Heart and the ego.

You: refers to the Being that gives life to the body. The lower-case "you" is the person.

The Absolute: that which you will never understand nor be able to define with your human mind.

Courage: human expression from the Heart.

I: free will: your power to act.

About the Author

A nne Astilleros is an internationally recognized speaker, workshops leader and life trainer with more than 25 years of experience awakening people to their own Reality. She is not only a true spiritual awakener but also a modern philosopher. Anne is the person behind Egolution, a Philosophy of Life. For more information on Anne please see her website *www.anneastilleros.com* or follow her on *facebook.com/anneastilleros*.